COLLABORATE AS IF YOUR LIFE DEPENDS ON IT

COLLABORATE AS IF YOUR LIFE DEPENDS ON IT

A GUIDE *to* WORKING TOGETHER *to* BE BETTER TOGETHER

DOUG CRAWLEY

LIONCREST
PUBLISHING

COLLABORATE AS IF YOUR LIFE DEPENDS ON IT
A Guide to Working Together to Be Better Together

ISBN   978-1-5445-0877-1 *Hardcover*
       978-1-5445-0876-4 *Paperback*
       978-1-5445-0875-7 *Ebook*

This book is dedicated to the important collaborations in my life:

To Dwight M. Kealoha ("K"), one of the finest individuals I have ever met, the best combat pilot with whom I ever flew, to whom I owe my life, who survived combat in Vietnam with me, who taught me the fundamentals of flying the RF-4C high-performance jet, and with whom these Five C's of collaboration were solidified. Thank you for still being my friend and for writing the foreword.

To Donald M. Stewart ("Stu"), one of my best friends for nearly forty years, the best pilot I've ever flown with in peacetime, who taught me the finer points of flying the RF-4C, by training me to fly as only instructor pilots were trained to do. You made us "better together."

To the other members of the Creek Circle Six (Melvin, Eddie, Bill, Deforest, and Bubba), with whom I first saw the Five C's of Collaboration in operation, even though I didn't realize it until so many years later. We simply called it "playing together."

To all the pilots with whom I was crewed (Ed Day, Dave Morgan, Glenn Bacchus, and Russ Alley), all the other pilots with whom I flew, and all the navigators who flew reconnaissance missions in Vietnam in the RF-4C.

To Mom and Dad (Sarah and Irving Fields), who reside in heaven and who first taught me that families working together are definitely "better together."

To my three sons (Tony, Geoff, and Rick) and my six grandkids (Adam, Langston, Miles, Aaron, Morgan, and Aiyanna). You continue to teach me how to collaborate with the younger generation.

To Shirley, who works with me, who helps me with the church, and who has collaborated with me for over thirty-five years. We call it a Godly marriage in which we have successfully blended our family. Thank you for loving me unconditionally, being my business partner, encouraging me in writing this book, and being the best wife that I could have.

To the team at Scribe who collaborated with me, especially Jenny Shipley, without whom I may not have ever completed this book.

Lastly, but by no means least, I would have never ended up where I am and learned what I have learned without being blessed by my Lord and Savior, Jesus Christ, with whom I collaborate in all areas of life.

CONTENTS

FOREWORD

How often does someone get to be part of an effort to create something of value for others? I have been given just that chance in writing this Foreword for Doug Crawley as he authors his book *Collaborate as If Your Life Depends on It*. While this book is about collaboration, it also is about Doug and his success in whatever endeavors he has pursued, including his experience as a Vietnam combat veteran flying out of Thailand in an RF-4C jet aircraft.

Doug will share with you some of the stories about the two of us—and the most interesting thing is to find us together more than fifty years later.

We met during the Vietnam War. Our squadron commander assigned us to work together, but I have no doubt that Doug and I would have found each other and become friends even without that assignment.

I was the only Hawaiian person and Doug was the only Black person in our squadron. In fact, Doug was the first Black man I knew. Growing up in Hawaii, I never saw all the differences or disparities in cultures. And in our collaboration, those differences simply didn't matter.

I was a pilot and he was a WSO—a weapons system officer. I sat in the front seat and he sat behind me, guiding us through our missions. Our relationship was like no other. We had a job to do, and our lives depended on us doing that job well—and working together. If we hadn't, we would have died.

I even taught Doug how to fly and land the airplane, just in case something happened—if I ever got shot or passed out—because I knew I could trust him to get us back home safely. That was unheard of in those days, but I had complete faith in him. I never had time to think about whether what we did required courage or not; I just knew that my commitment was to Doug and the Air Force.

If somebody had looked at us, two seemingly different crew members, and asked what allowed us to work so well together, I don't know if I could have put it into words. There are specific elements that lend themselves to a successful collaboration—and Doug covers those with the Five C's of Collaboration—but I certainly didn't know about them at the time.

For me, it all came down to trust and respect. I had respect for the person I was collaborating with, and I respected his ability to handle his side of the mission well. He had a talent for mission planning, mapping it out to figure out where we needed to go. I trusted that he knew where we were and would keep us heading in the right direction—beyond that, it was just a matter of me listening to him. I knew that if I depended on him to do the right thing, and he trusted that I would too, we would come back safely with the mission complete.

It didn't matter whether we flew at night or during the day, flying with Doug was a real treat. I had to watch out for him—but he was absolutely watching out for me too. We didn't work against each other; we just worked *together*.

After Doug and I finished our tour in Vietnam, we were stationed together at RAF Alconbury Air Force Base in England, but we split up there—he ended up with one squadron and I ended up in another. After a year or two, he was transferred and then he ended up leaving the service and taking a civilian job.

We lost touch after that, and I didn't hear from him for almost thirty years.

As it turns out, Doug was at home in New Jersey one day, talking with his son about the internet, and asked, "Can you find Dwight M. Kealoha on the internet?" His son looked me up, and later Doug and his wife got on an airplane and came to visit me and my wife in Hawaii where we instantly rekindled our long-lost friendship. We're able to sit and talk like no time at all had passed.

Even after all that time, Doug hasn't changed a bit. He's still the same great guy—honest, trustworthy, and with immense personal integrity.

He's also the absolute best person to write *Collaborate as If Your Life Depends on It*. Doug has lived and looked at life from many different vantage points—as a military officer, and a gentleman, as a pastor for his church, as a successful businessman, and as a husband, and a father.

Doug has learned through his experience that it does not matter whether you like somebody; it is more important that you become a part of a successful team with a common goal. His strength is in his ability to work together with other people, to take on challenges, and to listen so that people know they are heard. I've seen Doug in action, and he is a consummate professional. No matter the subject, he is the go-to guy when you need a leader.

To be honest, I don't have enough pages here to write all the good things I know about Doug; I could fill up a book just of our stories and experiences. Instead, I'll do just what I did back then: I'll turn the system over to Doug and trust him to get you safely where you need to go. You're in good hands.

Dwight "K" Kealoha
Brigadier General Officer, U.S. Air Force (retired)
CEO Hawaii Better Business Bureau (retired)

INTRODUCTION

"Russ, we're in a spin," I yelled from the back of our two-seat jet.

"Doug, we're below 10,000 feet," Russ, the front seat pilot yelled. "Get out. Eject! Eject! *Eject!*"

There was no further communication—and none was needed. In fact, I never even heard him say, "Eject." As soon as I recognized that we were in a spin—and the plane was going down—I started my ejection sequence.

We both were able to eject, the parachutes attached to our seats shot out automatically, and we were left swinging under the canopies as the airplane burned on the ground.

A few seconds later, and we wouldn't have gotten out.

I flew 185 missions during the Vietnam War, and if my pilot and I had not excelled at collaboration, I would not be alive to tell you my story.

I graduated from college in May of 1967. In July, I got a notice that I was to report to the Army on August 2nd. I knew I didn't want to join the Army, though, so on August 1st, I flew to basic training in San Antonio, Texas, to become an airman in the U.S. Air Force—even though that was my very first time in an airplane. I was going into the military to fly airplanes, but I didn't have a clue what it was all about.

Not long after I arrived, I was on the other side of the base when another soldier called my name and told me to leave the auditorium we were in and report back to my barracks. When I showed up, they said, "You're going to Officer's Training School."

One day I was in basic training to be an airman; the next, I was in class as an officer trainee.

I went to officer training school and later to flight school, learned to be a navigator, and graduated seventh out of thirty-five people. Because of that ranking, I got to choose what kind of airplane I wanted to fly, so I picked a high-performance jet. If I had chosen to fly a cargo plane, I probably wouldn't have gone to Vietnam—or, I would have just been going there, landing, and coming back. But the jet was glamorous. It was sleek, fast, and elite. Why would I drive a bus when I could choose a sports car instead? That jet was the epitome of flying!

I knew the basics of navigating a plane, but I had another stint at a more specialized flight school in Idaho to learn how to fly in the RF-4C high-performance jet and work with a pilot. I was assigned to be the navigator, with Major Ed Day as my pilot. We won the Top Crew award—just like in *Top Gun*, except we didn't have any guns, so they called it Top Crew instead—for being the number one crew in our class, based on our training missions.

After a year of "Nav" school and six months of training in Idaho, we went through sea survival, where they dropped us in the water in a little dinghy with shark repellant, so we could learn how to survive at sea. Then, arctic survival, where we had to crawl a couple of miles through the snow, under tripwire, cold, wet, and freezing. Then they put us in mock prisoner-of-war camps where they harassed and intimidated us—but though we were put in some very strenuous situations, they were still Americans, so I knew that nobody was going to do me bodily harm. Lastly, I went through jungle survival training, spending the night in a jungle in the Philippines, learning how to survive and evade capture if I ever got shot down over enemy territory.

Ultimately, Ed and I were stationed at the Udorn Royal Thai Air Force base in Thailand. Because of a change in his assignment, Ed was no longer able to fly on a regular basis. As a result, I was crewed with Dwight M. Kealoha, or K, a pilot from Hawaii, whom I had met when stationed in Idaho.

Together, K and I flew reconnaissance missions over Laos, Cambodia, and Vietnam—North and South.

MISSION: SURVIVAL

We often flew at night, in total darkness. We were at war, so people were shooting at us. The airplane we flew, the RF-4C, has been described as "the last *manned* tactical reconnaissance aircraft in the U.S. Air Force inventory." It was designed as a fighter aircraft with guns and bombs, but in our version those weapons were replaced with cameras so we could take photographs of military targets. Today, the military uses drones and satellites to take pictures of target sites, but back then that was our job—K flew the plane, and I sat in the back seat to navigate and operate the cameras. Flying reconnaissance has been described as the most dangerous job in the U.S. Air Force, and our mission's motto was "alone, unarmed, and unafraid."

All of the crews flying night missions received briefings before the flight, where they assigned us a set of targets.

As the navigator, I'd spend the hours between the briefing and takeoff planning the course K and I would fly on our night mission. The GPS, which was called the inertial navigation system, or INS, was only good to within two miles. Remember, this is 1969. I couldn't just put the coordinates in the computer and be led to the target. Using a paper map, I had to figure out which direction we wanted to go, based on the terrain—and determine points along that route that I would be able to identify on the radar. There were no lights on the ground, and if the stars weren't out, it was dark.

The only light came when I dropped the photo flash carts over the target. They made a huge flash that lit up the whole sky—but I could only use three for a given target. Any more than that and the enemy would know where we were, and where we were going from the pattern of flashes, and they would shoot us down.

The low-level flying part of the mission—flying in, getting shot at while trying to acquire pictures of those targets, and getting back to the base—only lasted a couple of hours…but those hours were dangerous.

There were missions where they would call us in the air with new targets, at night. While airborne, we had to figure out the route and then go fly it. K would get us in a holding pattern, and I'd take out my map and plan the mission in the air, using a small flashlight and the light from the radar screen to figure out our position and where to go. He couldn't see the map—or where we were going—so he was totally dependent on me.

We never saw other airplanes crash; people just wouldn't come back from their missions. We didn't know if they got shot down or not. We had no way of proving it, but we believed we lost as many or more people to running into the ground as to enemy fire. One mistake, on the part of either the pilot or the navigator, and we would crash.

When the enemy did start shooting at us, we could see the muzzle flashes. The tracers flew right by the cockpit. But we couldn't move or duck or do anything. K had to keep flying, and I had to turn the cameras on and keep reading the radar scope, sharing it with him when he needed it. We'd be flying and K would say to me, "Doug, they're shooting at us." I'd look up and say some words I don't use anymore then go back to what I was doing.

Most of the time, we couldn't see anything, and often we flew down in what's called karst, which is a rock formation that forms a valley we had to fly through. We were flying at 550 miles an hour 500 feet above the ground, so if K had turned at the wrong time, or if we got too close to the ground, we would have crashed— and died.

An article entitled "South Viet Nam: Eyes in the Sky," in the July 29, 1966 issue of *Time* magazine, quoted then-Captain Gale Hearn, an RF-4C pilot in the RVN who specialized in night flying, as saying, "We're more scared of those mountains than we are of the Viet Cong. You learn to trust your radar out there. When the moon goes down, it's like flying through an ink bottle."

The RF-4C was a tandem-seat jet, initially designed for two pilots, so there were controls in the back seat as well as in the front, allowing for either person to be able to fly the airplane. The dilemma in night flying, though, was that the radar system was designed such that we each had our own screen, but we could only utilize one mode at a time. I needed the Ground Mapping Mode ("GMM") of the radar to navigate, keep us on course, and ensure that we acquired the assigned target. But that mode only helped with directional navigation—it didn't say how high above the ground we were. K needed the Terrain Following Override ("TFO") mode of the radar to ensure that we didn't run into the ground, which we could not see. It didn't give any information about navigating, though.

At any given time, we could either know whether we were on course to the target or how high we were above the ground—but not both.

If we missed our targets, someone else had to risk their

lives to acquire the targets originally assigned to us. If we ran into the ground, we died and someone else would have to fly our mission. To make matters worse, when being shot at, we couldn't move the aircraft to avoid being shot down, because we had to stay on our planned course to the target.

The only solution was to time-share the radar system. K needed to keep us from crashing and I had to keep us on course. We had to work together and collaborate as if each of our lives depended on it, which, in fact, they did.

There was no "I" or "me" in that two-seat jet—there was only us. Because these night missions were so dangerous, we always flew with the same person we'd trained with—and had grown to trust our lives with. The men who flew those missions lived together, died together, won or lost together.

On a day mission, a colonel or another senior pilot could come down and ask to fly with me, and I'd fly in the back seat with him. But a night mission was only flown as a crew, just two of us, K and me.

We didn't try to get awards, though we did receive them, but only because somebody else decided that we should. We never fought each other; there was never any friction. If I said, "turn left to two-seven-five," K never replied with,

"You sure?" He just turned left to two-seven-five. It was the ultimate team effort.

We never thought we were heroes or doing anything that great; we were just doing our job—and we thought it was a great job to have. We both did our jobs well. We had been commissioned by the President of the United States. We knew we had done something that not everybody gets a chance to do.

COLLABORATE OR DIE?

Your life may not literally depend on your collaboration—like mine and K's did in that plane—but important aspects of your life might. Your job, your next promotion, your relationships, or even the success of your sports team may depend upon how well you can work together with the other people in your life.

Anytime we have two or more people doing anything together, we need to collaborate. And not collaborating well may hurt you or your company without you even realizing it.

When I go to the gym, I like to play pick-up basketball. Two guys are the captains, they choose teams, and we play against each other. We may have never played together—we may have never even seen each other before.

Can you imagine if professional sports teams operated the same way? If the NBA picked guys at random to be on teams and told them to just go out and play together, what kind of teamwork—or success—do you think they'd have?

Most businesses play pick-up ball. They put people on a team with no frame as to what their roles are or even what the overall goal is. There's no planning for collaboration, no training for it, and, as a result, everybody's just doing their own thing.

You may have experienced this yourself. Imagine you work for a publicly traded corporation, and you are expected to increase profits by 5 percent. You do what you were supposed to do, and you meet your quota, so everything's fine, right? As long as the marketing department gets what they need, and the design team takes care of what's important to them, and you hit your bottom line, the company profits.

But did you collaborate? Was it a team effort? Did you work together—with your clients, your team, and any other departments in your company—to be better *together*?

If someone reached out for help hitting their quota, did you raise them up so you could all do better, or are you like most people who say, "That's not my job?"

You're probably aware that there's a problem if you aren't

making your quota. But when you *are* hitting your targets, then you may not even be aware that things could be even better—and that's not your fault. Companies don't measure or track collaboration. We're never taught to work together effectively.

From our school years to our jobs to social situations, we are all just thrown together and expected to figure it out. Other than perhaps in the military or other professions where your life is on the line, like police or firefighters, most people never talk about how important collaboration is. Can you imagine if K and I hadn't been trained, if we had just been told to get in the airplane and go fly? "Make sure you work together, get the targets, and come back safely!" That would never work—but that's how collaboration is often approached, in the business world and in the rest of our lives.

What if the major business problem is not sales, revenue, expenses, the economy, or whatever else we can think it to be, but is in fact our inability to successfully collaborate?

I believe a lack of collaboration often lies at the foundation of failure. I want to open your eyes to how much better things can be when we all work together.

WORKING TOGETHER

As you now know, I'm a former Air Force captain. I'm also a black belt in Tae Kwon Do, a senior pastor in my church, and a husband, father, and grandfather. I am also the president and CEO of Synasha and Staffing Synergies, two companies with a 2019 combined revenue of over $100,000,000.

We have large companies as our customers, and sometimes a big corporation will claim to partner with us. There may be some element of partnership, but really most companies are doing what's best for them and telling us to adhere to their desires. True collaboration, however, would look like both partners getting in the same room and saying, "Let me share with you what my issues are, and you share with me what yours are. Let us understand exactly what you're trying to do, and if there's a way we can help you get there by working together, without hurting our team, let's make it happen."

Very few people do that. They sit in meetings together and they have conference calls. They may even believe they're collaborating, but most people do not have collaboration that's effective and makes life better.

We all have certain things in common: Everybody wants to feel appreciated if they go above and beyond the call of duty. People want to trust that their teammates will be there. If they're counting on you for something, they want to know that you'll come through.

If you are hitting your quota, but there's some inefficiency in your company that causes someone else not to hit their goals, the company suffers. When, instead, everybody works together to level out production, everyone does better without taking away from anybody.

When we learn how to collaborate effectively, efficiency improves, and total value increases. Rather than there being one star or standout performer and everybody else looking out for number one, working together better brings everybody to a higher level—together.

Whether in a marriage, ministry, or in the military, most people enjoy working with other team players. Working together well makes your collaboration more pleasant, sure, but it also reassures you that you can count on the other person in a crunch or crisis situation. You feel that respect. You enjoy working together more, and you overcome adversity better. And as a result, your company, relationship, or other collaborations become more efficient—and more successful.

When you're working with people you trust and respect, you want to go that extra step because you care about how it will affect them. Basically, when a team wins, everybody wins.

THE FIVE C'S OF COLLABORATION

Collaboration is a word with many meanings. On a team, it can mean working together. In labor relations, it's an agreement. Military aviation refers to it as "crew coordination." It's called love in a marriage, brotherhood in a fraternity, and unity in the church—but all of these terms are referring to the same thing: collaboration.

We do very few things by ourselves, and the major things in life involve working together with someone else if we want to be successful. I've come up with a system to improve collaboration anywhere it occurs, at every level, and I call it the Five C's of Collaboration:

- Commitment
- Clarity
- Confidence
- Caution
- Courage

All Five C's are important, and we need all of them for effective collaboration. But what you're going to see in the next chapter, which will give you more of an overview of the Five C's, is that the first three—commitment, clarity, and confidence—set the foundation for the other two, caution and courage.

Because these three are essential to collaboration, reading

those three chapters is the minimum you need to begin working together better. I recommend reading them in order, from chapter 1 through chapter 6, and then reading the conclusion to see when collaboration truly saved my life. Reading all of the chapters will take your understanding to a higher level.

Improving your collaborations may not save your life, but it certainly will change it.

NOTES FROM A PANDEMIC

When I developed the title and started writing this book, I had no idea that America and the world at large would soon need to collaborate at such an extreme level—but that is exactly where the coronavirus and our inability and unwillingness to cooperate has brought us.

Preachers often tell a well-known parable about a man who said to God one day, "God, I would like to know what heaven and hell are like." In response, God showed the man two doors.

When the door to the first room opened, the man saw a large pot of stew in the middle of the room. It smelled delicious and was incredibly appetizing; his mouth started to water right away. However, when he looked closer, the man saw that the people in the room were thin, sickly, despondent, and seemed to be starving. Each person had a spoon with a long handle attached to both of their hands. They could easily reach into the pot and get a spoonful of stew—but because the handle was longer than their arms, they couldn't put the spoonful of stew into their mouths. As a result, everyone in the room was hungry and suffering.

God said to the man, "You have now seen hell."

Then God opened the second door, and initially everything appeared to be exactly the same as in the first room. There was the same pot of stew. There were the same long-handled spoons attached to the hands of the people. But in this room, the people were fit, well-fed, talking and laughing, having fun, and upbeat.

God said to the man, "You have now seen heaven."

The man replied, "I don't understand."

God smiled and said, "It's simple—the people here work together and feed one another, while those in hell only think of themselves."

Could it be that the difference between heaven and hell on earth is our ability to work together?

The collaborative response to the pandemic has been newsworthy and sometimes praiseworthy, but it has been far from perfect. Individual states and FEMA have fought against each other for ventilators, the stock market is dropping then jumping back up unpredictably, unemployment is rising, and hospitals are running out of PPE. States locked down, then began to reopen again—and the virus is still out there, claiming lives.

We are left with so many questions yet to be answered: Will we ever get back to normal? How will we protect the medical professionals and first responders? Will the government provide adequate help to businesses and individual citizens? Can the economy rebound quickly? Can we get enough tests? Will a vaccine be developed soon? Will I become infected? Will I or my loved ones die? Will medical professionals have to decide who gets healthcare and who does not? Will we come out of this united or divided? How do we keep food in the food banks when meat packing plants are closing, farmers are pouring out milk on the ground, and crops are going to waste?

How can we address the pandemic issues we are facing? We can collaborate as if our lives depend on it—because they quite literally do. How are we to do this? Read this book and devise and implement a plan, based on what you learn. Then work together to be better together.

> Never in recent times have we been so dependent on each other, which is why now, more than ever, we *must* work together. The degree to which we collaborate will determine whether we thrive...or simply survive.

BETTER TOGETHER

This book applies to everybody. We all have to work together with *someone* at *some* point.

As good as hall-of-fame quarterback, John Elway was, he couldn't do it by himself—or with a team of people thrown together on the playing field. He needed a team working together to block for him, to pass him the ball without fumbling it, to catch the ball when he threw it, and to play defense so he could get back out on that field.

The issue is not *will* you collaborate or *should* you collaborate—it's how successful will you be when you inevitably have to work together with someone?

If you are a fan of a winning professional sports team, you've probably seen them apply the Five C's. If you're married or in a relationship, the Five C's apply to you, too. If you're the leader of a business organization, they apply. If you're a pastor, a player, a parent, guess what? The Five C's of Collaboration can help you too.

You have the opportunity to work together better, on all these different levels, with all these different people.

We each have our own personal, specific set of circumstances where improved collaboration can drastically improve our lives. It would be impossible for me to include every possible opportunity for collaboration in a book. But if you look at where you are and your life's details—where you work, who you live with, the people you encounter every day—you can take the Five C's and apply them to your life with amazing results.

I'll guide you through the Five C's on a higher level, and then you can put them into action in your life and see what a difference it will make when we're all better together.

CHAPTER 1

——

AN OVERVIEW OF THE FIVE C'S OF COLLABORATION

Two sisters are fighting over an orange. The mother intervenes, frustrated with the fighting, and cuts the orange in half, giving one half to each sister.

The first sister goes into her room, peels the orange, throws the peel away, and eats the fruit. The second sister is baking a cake, so she goes into the kitchen, grates the peel into her cake, and throws away the rest.

If they had only collaborated, they each could have had twice as much!

I am not suggesting that collaboration will always result

in our getting twice as much. But what if we increased revenue and profits by 20 percent? What if our marriages improved by 30 percent? What if a professional sports team improved by 10 percent?

NO MAN (OR WOMAN) IS AN ISLAND

I am a black belt at Tae Kwon Do, which may seem like an individual sport, but I had to work with my instructor over a long period of time to get to that level. Simone Biles, on the US Olympic gymnastics team may perform alone, but she has teammates, coaches, trainers, doctors, and a whole team of people she works with that led to Olympic gold.

According to the 2017 Great Place to Work Report, "Concern over competition for talent has become a driving force, and creative collaboration has become essential in the face of fast-paced change."[1]

If we look at a relay team, each person runs 100 meters before passing the baton to their teammate; no single runner can outrun a relay team. The fastest runner of the 400-meter dash can't run faster than four people each running 100 meters.

---

[1] "Three Predictions for the Workplace Culture of the Future," Great Place to Work, accessed September 5, 2020, https://www.greatplacetowork.com/images/reports/Fortune_100_Report_2017_FINAL.pdf.

No one person is responsible for the success or failure; it's that set of four people working together that's going to lead to their results. There's no prize for running the fastest individual time—and if you're the fastest but you drop the baton during the handoff, you're most likely going to lose the race. Medals are awarded only to the team with the fastest overall time.

If we bring this example back into the business world, you may have one person who outperforms everyone else in a certain area, but if he or she can't work together with the rest of the team, then that individual's contribution doesn't have the same impact that it would with a full team of people all working their best together.

When companies hire new employees, they have the tendency to focus on the individual talent, education, and experience of the employee. Do they have a master's degree in business? Have they worked in the industry? No matter how much of that experience matches expectations, if they can't work with the team, they don't have a good employee.

Even if that candidate makes it to an interview, they may be tested on many things—but they aren't being tested on working together. Yet collaboration is even *more* important in today's environment. Most companies don't have offices like they used to. Modern work spaces mean you bring your computer and sit somewhere different every day, with the idea that people who are closer together can work together. To reach success, however, we must take it a step further: we need to not just work together but work together *better*.

If a customer and a supplier really collaborate, each one can have more than they currently do—rather than each looking out for their own best interest, as we saw in the illustration that opened this chapter.

BETTER TOGETHER

We all have to work with people. And in every area of life—from ministry to marriage, business to baseball—there can be catastrophic consequences when we fail to collaborate.

When we're not working together, sports teams lose. Marriages end in divorce or lead to unhappy people staying together in unsatisfying situations. Churches split. In business, failure to collaborate impacts the top line and the bottom line—and sometimes leads to the demise of the entire company. When we see businesses go bankrupt, some of that may be attributed to the fact that they didn't work together well enough to anticipate the change in the market.

If, for example, cab companies were working together to plan, predict, and prepare for changes to their industry, they should have been the ones to come up with the concept of ride sharing. They didn't, however, and Uber and Lyft disrupted the whole taxi industry.

But when collaboration is improved, not only are those catastrophes avoided but the opposite happens: we become stronger.

Marriages are successful, even through the inevitable challenges, and the people involved get along and grow together. At work, efficiency improves. In fact, McKinsey states that "innovative business collaboration can increase your company's productivity by 20 to 30 percent."[2]

Too often, we see churches where the focus is on the individual pastor, who is put on a pedestal by the membership. The pastor is the sole leader and the members are the followers. But biblical leadership was never to be that way. Biblical leadership is servant or shared leadership. It is meant to be a group of leaders serving the congregation. In fact, the best (and often largest) churches are organized in this way, with smaller groups collaborating to make the church function properly.

---

2   "Technology, Media & Telecommunications," McKinsey & Company, accessed September 5, 2020, https://www.mckinsey.com/industries/high-tech/ how-we-help-clients/impact-stories/innovative-collaboration-techniques- improve-productivity-across-global-teams.

When I founded the church where I serve as pastor, I was the sole leader. But as soon as I could, I identified other potential leaders and eventually ordained them as deacons and elders. Our church would never have functioned properly, or became what it is, if I had remained the only leader.

Sports teams benefit from improved collaboration, too.

My favorite basketball player is Steph Curry, on the Golden State Warriors. He's changed the game. He shoots better than anybody I've ever seen—and I've been playing the game for more than sixty-five years.

The reason the Warriors win more than some other teams (when everybody's not hurt, that is) is because they play team ball. The individual players are willing to sacrifice for the team. Steph Curry is the only unanimous Most Valuable Player in the history of the NBA, but when Kevin Durant, who is another of the best players in the NBA, came to play for the Warriors, Steph Curry sacrificed part of his game. He didn't take quite as many shots, he wasn't the focal point most of the time, but he did that so the team could win.

The Warriors had Steph Curry, Kevin Durant, Klay Thompson, who may be the second best shooter behind Steph Curry, and Draymond Green, who was Defensive Player of the Year in 2017—and they all worked together to win rather than looking out for their own individual stats—or salaries. Kevin Durant even agreed to take less money so they could afford to keep everyone else on the team.

What's best for the team can be more important than what's best for you as an individual. If you work hard by yourself and raise your average to shooting thirty-five points a game, the team can still lose. But if you all work together, even if you only average twenty-five points a game, the team can win.

When everybody only looks out for themselves, you won't have a successful team effort. I'm not saying that people can't do what they're best at—they absolutely should—but sometimes they have to *not* be the star player or the MVP of the team or of the company because it's what's best for everyone.

A great team is not made up of one great star, but of great teammates. Winning teams are ones where everybody puts the team first. And teams that work together based on the Five C's of Collaboration are better together.

THE HOUSE THAT COLLABORATION BUILT

Imagine a simple, five-sided house, like one a child might draw. It probably looks something like this:

CAUTION

COURAGE

**Collaborate As If
Your Life Depends On It**

*Working Together To
Be Better Together*

CLARITY

CONFIDENCE

COMMITMENT

If we look at this pentagon-shaped outline of the house, the bottom line—the foundation—represents commitment. Without a foundation, a house isn't going to stand. Similarly, if you don't have that commitment, the rest of your collaboration isn't going to work.

The house is then framed by the load-bearing walls of clarity and confidence. Without them, the house cannot be built. In collaboration, once you're committed to something, you need to clearly understand the mission, the goal, and what your role is—you need clarity. Then, you have to have enough confidence in the process and in the other people you're collaborating with to know that they'll do what they're supposed to do—and that you will, too.

If you take out any one of these first three C's, the whole thing falls apart. Remove commitment, clarity, or confidence, and you get a whole new C: chaos.

Finally, the house is finished with the roof of caution and courage. It's important to first build commitment, clarity, and confidence; there's nothing for the roof to rest on if you don't. Once you've done that, you can add to your collaboration by bringing in caution and courage, which will make that collaboration better and safer.

Caution gets you to think through the potential dangers and difficulties of your situation. It's not enough to just think about what you have to do. You also have to predict potential pitfalls, anticipate where the plan may go wrong, and avoid taking unnecessary risks.

You don't want to let caution hold you back, though. You still need the courage to move forward. Once you identify the potential risks and pitfalls, you need the courage to confront them should they become a reality. Murphy was right—there are going to be obstacles. Adversity will always exist, and people are always afraid of something.

Choosing to let go of or move past these fears allows you to finally be open to full collaboration.

With courage, your collaboration is going to move forward in spite of those things that try to hold you back—and in spite of your fear.

That fear is why you need to start the process with commitment. When you're committed to your collaboration, you're not going to say, "Oh man, that mission is too dangerous. I'm not going to do that!"

But commitment alone is not enough—we have to be committed to the right things in the right way. So we also need clarity—clarity of your role, of the mission—because you and the people you're working with have to be in agreement on what you're trying to accomplish and how you're going to get there. But commitment and clarity alone are not enough, either. We also need confidence in each other, in our own skillset, in leadership, and in the tools necessary for successful completion of the assignment.

Additionally, we need caution so that we know when it's time to pivot or when it's time to abort before we exceed the allotted time, the availability of resources, or the collective human capabilities.

Finally, we need courage to give us the willingness to do what we're committed to do, what we're clear about and have confidence in, even in the face of adversity. To have successful collaboration, we need a culture of commitment, clarity, confidence, caution, and courage.

BULLSEYE

One farmer goes out to another farmer's farm and looks at the side of the barn. He sees all these arrows right in the middle of the bullseyes. He asks the other farmer, "How did you get to be such a good archer? You make every single shot!"

The other farmer says, "I shoot the arrow first, and then I paint the bullseye around the arrow!"

Much like that farmer, we call working with people, collaboration, but we're actually painting the target around the arrow. We're calling things a success…after the fact.

When you apply the Five C's of Collaboration to your specific situation—and those specifics are going to be different for each business, ministry, marriage, or team—you'll then have a process that will lend itself to working together successfully. You'll be shooting bullseyes, no paint required.

INNOVATION AND COLLABORATION

Collaboration and innovation often go hand in hand. Companies say they're going to collaborate for innovation, but innovation is a process, not a goal.

Often, companies put people together and tell them to come up with *something*. Sometimes that works, and the people are able to innovate and come up with something good. More often than not, however, it doesn't work because there's no commitment. There's no clarity. And, thus, there's no confidence.

Sticking people in a room and saying, "I want you guys to form a team and be innovative and come up with something that will disrupt the industry," doesn't work any better than throwing all those people together and saying, "Collaborate!"

The focus has to be on *how* you innovate—just as this book's focus is on *how* you work together. Again, innovation is a process, not a goal—and so is collaboration. Companies may say, "Our goal is collaboration," but working together is not a destination. You don't say, "Okay, we collaborated—we're done!"

A certain, specific collaboration may end, but the process of collaboration is ongoing. It's something that you work on, that you continue to put in place, and that you continue to improve upon. As long as we need other people, we need to be able to work together.

In the military, for example, they didn't just give us an airplane and say, "Okay, you're going to go fly in combat now."

Collaboration didn't start during the mission, or when we got to the airplane, or even when we arrived for a preflight briefing. It started months and years before, with school and training. It started in a classroom before we were even crewed up and certainly before we got in the airplane. Both K and I had college degrees and had been trained as USAF officers. We had flight training, navigation training, training on our specific airplane, and survival schools—all before we ever stepped foot in Southeast Asia or flew a combat mission. I joined the Air Force in August of 1967 and didn't fly combat until September of 1969.

In our years of training, we learned to work together at so many different points before we were up there, in the air, flying our missions.

I could look back and say, "Okay, we flew successful missions, therefore we collaborated well."

It is true that we collaborated well—but that would be painting the bullseye around the arrow. Instead, we have to look back and see the whole successful process of collaboration that led to that point.

Working together is more important than most companies or individuals realize. I don't think most organizations recognize how often they're painting the target around the arrow. They say, "We made $100,000 this month, we're a success," but they don't realize that perhaps with the right process in place they could have made five times as much.

I recently had a meeting with a large pharmaceutical company who has a great product that's selling really well in Europe, and that they think is going to be tremendously successful here in the United States. My company doesn't make the devices; we put them together into packages.

I had to have the same conversation with them that I've had with so many other companies. If they give us the components and ask us to bid on the job, the only thing we can compete on is price. But if we collaborate from the beginning—at least having a discussion earlier in the supply chain process—there are things that can be done to make the whole process more efficient, leading to an even lower price in the end. We can help them design the packaging and help them save money on materials and assembly.

A product is considered successful if it gets to market

on time, but the process to get it there could have been even easier. If the marketing department is only concerned about marketing, and the design team is only concerned about the design, people are not working together—and that company is going to pay more to get this product out than they should. Until the whole company works together and removes some of those silos, to be able to see some of those inefficiencies, everybody is just going to keep doing what they're doing.

I don't just want you to learn how to work together so we can all be friends and hold hands and sing "Kumbaya." If any of that happens, great—but that's not the point. The point is to learn to work together—to be able to reduce inefficiencies, to maximize profit, to help your business (or other collaboration) remain successful *and* become a better place to work. When that happens, we can all be better together.

If you don't already have a process in place for collaboration, for training your team to work together, that's okay. The rest of this book is going to show you how to get started on that training and how to put this process in place *now* so that you have it when you need it.

COMING UP WITH THE FIVE C'S

One day, I was talking with one of the guys I flew with

and I said, "You know, what we did when we were flying combat was really the epitome of collaboration."

He agreed, and I began thinking about the particular elements that made us successful—that's when God gave me the beginning of the idea of these Five C's based on the mission I flew.

The first time I flew combat in the airplane, I was committed. I knew what I needed to do, and I was confident that K did too...but I'd never been in combat before. We went out, and I saw the Five C's in action—and that reinforced their importance. Each time we were successful, it built more clarity, more confidence, even more caution and courage—and that built upon our foundation of commitment.

I began to look at different scenarios, to see if they applied. I thought about winning the city championship when I was a kid (which you'll read about in chapter 4), and I could see that we had used the Five C's then. I thought about starting a church and playing basketball in the Senior Olympics—the Five C's applied in those situations, too. When I started my businesses, when my wife and I got married, even as I wrote this book—in all of these different scenarios, I recognize the pattern of the Five C's being present.

I had to commit to this idea. Then I had to gain clarity around it and have confidence in it. I exhibited caution by running through each of those scenarios to make sure the Five C's actually applied in each instance. And now I'm having the courage to embrace the concept and bring it out into the world.

But it all started with commitment, and that's what we're going to look at in the next chapter.

EXERCISE

At the end of each chapter, I've included a question or series of questions you can ask yourself to thoroughly absorb and process the chapter content. Feel free to write your answers right in the book!

Think of the greatest example of teamwork or collaboration that you have seen or heard of in business, in sports, in the military, and in marriage. What makes each great?

CHAPTER 2

THE FIRST C: COMMITMENT

One day on the farm, the animals decide that they're going to make a meal for the farmer to thank him for taking such good care of them.

"Let's fix breakfast for the farmer," says the chicken. "I'll give you some eggs."

"Okay," says the cow. "Here's what I'll do: I'll give you some milk for the breakfast."

They both look at the pig.

"Now hold on a second," the pig says. "You guys are making a contribution, but you're asking me to make a commitment!"

THE FOUNDATION

As we established in the previous chapter, commitment is the foundation of collaboration. If you don't have that, everything else falls apart.

If you build a house over a fault line and the foundation cracks, it doesn't matter how well you build the walls and how much attention you give the roof—the building is going to be unstable. Similarly, the other four C's are extremely important, but if the people involved in the collaboration are not committed to it, nothing else matters, because it's not going to work.

One of the reasons the military works so well is because the people in it are committed. You don't take a hill under enemy fire or fly through the dark with the risk of crashing if you're not committed to what you're doing. The epitome of commitment is when your life depends on it.

But what is commitment?

Commitment means that you have some skin in the game. When you are committed, you're willing to do whatever it takes to work together for the outcome that you're looking for. Commitment is not a process; it's a decision to go all in. Your commitment is not just to the mission; part of your commitment is to prepare or train for that mission. You don't have to wait until you've actually flown the mission to believe that you can do what you're supposed to. You go through training, you take tests, you've been in the simulator. You're committed to seeing that mission through long before you actually fly it.

And when your collaboration has that level of commitment—along with the other four C's we'll talk about in upcoming chapters—your probability of being successful in what you're trying to accomplish increases exponentially.

When I was in the military, that commitment to training, to going to briefings, to learning everything we could came from the fact that our lives were literally on the line. We didn't know when the airplane might catch fire, or if the hydraulics system was going to stop working. We didn't know if we were going to have to eject—but we knew that it was a possibility, and we took our commitment seriously.

Your life may not be at risk, but your commitment comes from the high stakes of what matters in your life. That's why the first step in evaluating your commitment to collaboration is to ask yourself what's at stake.

STEP ONE: CONSIDER THE CONSEQUENCES

When we were flying combat, it was easy to realize that our lives were on the line. Sometimes it's more difficult to consider the consequences in other areas of life.

If you're not committed to collaborate well in your marriage, what's at stake? Your relationship. If a husband cheats on his wife, it might feel good in the moment, but has he sat down and thought through the consequences? What's the worst that could happen? Well, you could get a divorce. You might have to move out of the house. You're no longer able to see the kids, especially when she moves three states away to be closer to her family. When you look at it that way, you can see how much is on the line.

If you're on a basketball team and you're not committed to the team—showing up to practice late, not hustling back down the court, or showing up out of shape—you might sit on the bench all season and not get to play. You could end up getting traded or even cut.

If you're not committed at work—showing up late, leaving early, doing the bare minimum and dismissing the rest with, "that's not my job"—your promotion or even your job may be at stake. But you don't just want to be committed at the higher levels—there are consequences of not committing to working together better in every interaction, for every aspect of business. Those may be higher costs, greater inefficiencies, lost time, or wasted money.

What's at stake may be not doing what's best for your business, your company, or your customers. It may be not doing what's best for your family or for your marriage.

Collaboration is necessary for all of us, which means that your lifestyle—the way you live your life—is at stake. You may not literally die, because you can go find another job to keep a roof over your head and food on the table, but you are still going to have to collaborate in any job you have. And ultimately, we're all working to support ourselves and our families, to provide that roof, that food, and that stability. So in a very real way, our lives *are* at stake—just not in the immediate sense, as it would be for a first responder or someone in the military.

If you're a corporate executive living in the suburbs, and you lose your job, ultimately because of your lack of collaboration, your lifestyle and that of your loved ones are at risk. You have to go home and tell your daughter that she has to leave her private school and go to public school, that you have to move because you can't afford to stay in that house any longer. The circumstances may not be life-threatening, but they are life-altering.

There's a lot at stake for everyone to be able to collaborate well and, again, that first step is commitment. When you recognize just how much is at stake, it can help solidify your commitment to better collaboration, because you're committing to not let that consequence occur. And if you commit as if your life depends on it, you have a higher probability of having a positive outcome.

STEP TWO: EXAMINE THE BENEFITS

Next, ask yourself what the benefits of committing to the collaboration are. What do you get out of this commitment? What makes it worth it to you?

If your life literally depends on your commitment to this collaboration, it's pretty easy to identify the benefit: if you don't do it, you might die. If what's at stake is what you risk losing—your marriage, your job, your lifestyle—the benefit is the positive gain commitment to the collaboration brings.

Going back to our marriage example, we've examined what the consequences are if it doesn't work—but what could it be like if it *does* work? What if you can live happily ever after with a marriage made in heaven? Your heart still skips a beat every night when you come home. You want to grow old together. You look forward to building your dream house and having children. Even when things are difficult—and there are always going to be ups and downs—you take comfort, pride, and joy in the partner you have by your side.

Spend as much time considering how good your successful collaboration can be as you spent thinking about how bad it will be if you don't commit.

Only once you know both of these answers, and you've

clearly identified the positives and negatives, can you make your decision to commit.

STEP THREE: MAKE YOUR DECISION TO COMMIT

People ask me for my secret to being as old as I am and still going to the gym and playing basketball with teenagers and younger men. I tell them that I don't have a secret but that I stay in shape by treating exercise like I do my job.

You don't wake up and say, "You know what? I don't feel like working today—I'll go tomorrow." (Particularly not if you work for someone else!) You just get up and you go to work. The same thing is true with exercise—or anything else you're committed to. You put it on your schedule, and you do it.

I love playing basketball in the local gyms and in senior tournaments around the country. I'm committed to playing basketball. I don't like lifting weights, but I am also committed to doing so approximately twice a week because it helps me maintain strength and muscle tone. I do it simply because I need to do it for me and my teams to be successful.

When you're really committed, you are passionate about it. You *want* to do it. Not only are you willing to do it, you feel good about doing it.

But if you're not committed, it becomes, "Well, maybe I'll do it tomorrow or two days from now..."

When I was in college, we had to take PE as one of our mandatory classes. My PE teacher was also the track coach, and I was a pretty decent runner, so he told me, "You have a B in the class right now, but if you join the track team, you'll get an A."

If you look at my college yearbook, you'll see me in the photograph with the track team—but I never ran a single race. My heart wasn't in it—you had to run long distances every day, even on some weekends. I wanted the A, but I wasn't committed to doing what was necessary in order to be good at track. I didn't go all-in on my decision. If I had been committed, I would have run anyway because I was committed to the effort, to doing what's best for the team—just like I am now with basketball.

I go to the gym every week and shoot the basketball. I play two or three times a week. I watch videos, I've played (and won!) in the Senior Olympics, and I've even been to fantasy camps with NBA players like Dwayne Wade, Kevin Durant, and Coach K, who coaches Duke and is the former coach of the USA Olympic team. My heart is in basketball, and it was easy to commit to playing.

Once you've made your decision and you're committed,

you can't rely on commitment alone. Now, you have new decisions to make as part of fulfilling your commitment: decisions around leadership and teamwork, planning and preparation, training and practice.

LEADERSHIP, PREPARATION, TRAINING, AND TEAMWORK

When my wife and I moved to New Jersey for my new job in 1986, I had only preached two sermons in my life, but I felt the calling to become a pastor.

As a result of the move, I joined a church in New Jersey and volunteered for a couple years as an associate minister. Then I went to another church for a couple of years as an associate minister. I hadn't been academically trained in ministry, so I started going to school, attending seminars, and learning how to preach better.

I interviewed with and ended up as the pastor of a traditional Baptist church in New Jersey, but it was tough because the leadership didn't want to do very much to impact the local community, such as having an after-school program.

At that time, my wife and I were both working in higher-paying consulting jobs. It was only after a period of extended unemployment for each of us that we had moved to New Jersey for jobs—when you're desperate, you'll go just about anywhere, and New Jersey had become home. I traveled out of state to locations in Texas, Virginia, and Washington, DC, worked during the week and spent nights writing sermons, and weekends preaching and pastoring. One Sunday, I preached and, afterwards, I thought to myself, *Doug, you really did not prepare that sermon as well as you should have.*

No one else could tell, but I knew the truth: I was trying to do too much—and I wasn't committed enough to be able to do both consulting and pastoring well.

So, with my wife's blessing, I quit my consulting job, going from six figures annually to making $500 a month. Knowing this, the congregation voted to give me a raise. The church operated under congregational rules, so the people voted on everything, but even so, the leadership refused to implement the raise. They were more concerned about how much money the church had in the bank than how much of an impact we could have in the community.

I ended up resigning from that church, but about ten of us talked about the possibility of starting our own church—a non-denominational church that would support some of our goals with the community. Starting a church from scratch required a lot of collaboration—and serious commitment, too.

Initially, the church was basically in the trunk of my family car. Sunday services were held in the local elementary school, where we rented space. We'd go to the school on Sundays, take everything out and set it up, I'd preach, and then we'd put it back in the trunk of the car and go home.

I put this group together so when we started the church, I wasn't just the pastor—I became *everything*. I had to make all the decisions. I know myself, and I knew I wasn't going to do anything wrong on purpose, but I didn't want even the appearance of any wrongdoing. We needed strong leadership and I couldn't do it all myself. So rather than set up congregational rules, we decided to have elders in the church for shared leadership. As early as possible, I started training people to become elders. The congregation would observe them for a year or so, to make sure they were really prepared, and then we ordained them as elders. As we grew, so did our church structure—adding deacons and deaconesses.

I still give a sermon in that same church on most Sundays, and several members of the congregation have been with us since the beginning. Some of the kids whose dedications I performed when they were babies are now college graduates with master's degrees.

We're not a large church, but we are a church that has a large impact on the community. We feed families outside of the church during the Christmas holiday season. We give out backpacks at the beginning of the school year to kids from low-income families. We have an after-school program, with a basketball court and gym equipment, and we open the gym for members and others to exercise.

For several years, we operated a free six-week summer program for local kids to receive instruction in reading, math, social behavior, Spanish, English, and the Bible. We hired college students, who needed summer jobs, as teachers and assistants in the program. We also fed the students who attended. The church provided volunteers and space, and the funds to pay students and teachers were provided by my businesses. We were committed to making a difference.

SAME GOES FOR BUSINESS

In a business organization, as teams are formed, employees should be committed to their team, to applying the Five C's, and to being successful at their jobs. But nothing will happen in a business environment unless leadership first buys into it. Without the support of management and leaders behind the collaboration, success is incredibly unlikely.

Whether you're the employee, the manager, or the leader herself, collaboration will be difficult to make happen without commitment to that collaboration that's driven from the top. You have to be committed from the top down if you are ultimately going to be successful.

In 2019, I went to a summit for companies that work directly with minority-owned suppliers. As you can imagine, there was a lot of talk about diversity and why it's so important. It's good business sense to have diverse thought on a team, so a lot of companies say, "We want diversity."

Companies say they're committed to that diversity, but the companies that have the most success are the ones where someone in leadership—the CEO or chairman of the board—says, "Diversity is important. It is our goal, and we're going to track our progress toward that goal." And, puts those words into action.

That may mean giving money to organizations that certify minority business enterprises, evaluating how many minority suppliers the procurement manager is using, or asking an HR manager for the makeup of the workforce population—not for quotas, but to evaluate the whole company's commitment to diversity, from the top down.

DICTATORS NOT WELCOME

Commitment to leadership will work as long as you are a leader, not a dictator. This holds true in relationships as well as in business.

I take a biblical perspective of marriage, and it's clear that the husband is the head of the household. I'm married to a strong woman, and we make decisions together. In fact, she controls all the finances because she's better at it than I am. But occasionally we have a conflict and I'll exercise my authority. When our younger son needed to leave college and move back home, we had a hard time agreeing on whether or not he would come live with us. Eventually, I said, "That's the way it's going to be." And she would agree now that it was the right decision.

If I were just a dictator and she had to do everything I said to do, that wouldn't be collaboration. I'm not in charge of everything. I don't tell her what to do. I don't even do that at the office, and it's my company! I don't walk around saying, "You better do what I say."

I am committed to the success of those collaborations—at work and at home—so I am a leader. And leadership, again from a biblical perspective, is servant leadership, whether as a pastor or in the family. Rather than one guy at the top telling everybody else what to do, there's one person at the bottom serving everybody else. It's a different type of leadership that can help reduce, if not eliminate, a lot of concerns because it highlights the leader's commitment to doing what's best overall.

WORKING TOGETHER

Teamwork means that you're committed to working together. You've made a decision, and you don't have time—particularly when flying combat—to say, "I don't like you," or, "I don't care for that tone of voice."

You have to work together, so you're not going to talk to somebody in a way that threatens that commitment.

Over the years in my relationships, I've learned to pick my battles and when to just let stuff go. I'm committed, so why would I want to fight about something that's not a big deal?

Because we're all so different, we have to work at collaboration. If we were all the same, it'd be easy. We'd understand where everybody was coming from, there'd be no misunderstandings, and we'd all know how to anticipate what the other person wants or needs.

But whether in a marriage, at work, in the military, on a sports team, or in a ministry, we are all different people who have different backgrounds and different wants and needs. Learning to be committed to the goal *no matter what* allows us to figure out how to work together, how to make this collaboration work while thinking about other people—*because* we have made a commitment.

The people I flew with came from all different backgrounds—different parts of the country, different schools, different races, and different experiences. I was a Black man from the South; K was from Hawaii. No matter what, we were expected to collaborate, and no matter our background, we were committed to that.

PLANNING AND PREPARATION

Once you've made your decision to true commitment, your focus is now on doing the best job you can—*because* you're committed.

But deciding to commit to making something happen doesn't just automatically make it happen. Just because you accept a job offer doesn't mean you're doing the job—you still have to commit to showing up every day, learning how to do the job well, preparing for your project, seeing it through, and doing the best job that you can.

Part of that commitment process is committing to the team or the job, and with that comes preparation and planning. Now you have to focus on that which you're committed to.

Personal commitment means having a willingness to do more than just the basic requirements of the job. You're committed to going above and beyond the call of duty.

You're committed to continuous learning—reading books and taking courses to support your new position.

As a pastor of a church, I perform wedding ceremonies for my church members and family. But I would never agree to marry any couple if they didn't go through premarital counseling first, to show that not only are they committed to this union but that they're *prepared* for it as well.

Once, I sat down with a couple and asked the guy, "Do you know her financial situation?" He didn't have a clue that she had $100,000 in student loans!

I ask couples, "How are you going to raise the children?" "Who's going to be in charge of the finances?" I talk through marriage with the couple to be wed and have them think through what is essential to making their relationship work. That way, when they get married, that's not the first time they've ever discussed how they will work together.

Marriage is one of the most important things we do in life, but a lot of times people fall in love and just decide to get married. But we all need some preparation, some training—even in a marriage—to learn how to work together well.

TRAINING AND PRACTICE

In business, we want people to work together well, and we expect that to just happen by putting them in the same office. Without any training, companies tell new employees to work on a team with the people who are already there. And that sets us up for failure.

As we've discussed, almost everything we do in business—and in life—involves working together with other people. But, other than in the military and on sports teams, we don't train people on *how* to work together.

If you don't train people, it's very difficult to have good teamwork.

I play basketball with several firemen, and I asked one of the players, "You have three guys on an engine and two on the back, some guys get the water hose and other guys turn it on, you have the driver of the truck…how do you all learn to work together?"

He replied, "We start out working together."

Organizations like the fire department, police department, the military—places where people put their lives on the line at work—train people *while* they're working together.

When I play pickup ball, I often don't have a clue about

the other guys I play with. I don't know whether he goes left or right, whether he can shoot outside or if he's quick and can go to the basket. When I play on an organized team, however, we've identified who's the center, the forward, who can play down low or shoot outside. But we don't make that decision on the court—we do that in training and practice.

It's no different in business. You're committed to working for a company, but you also need to be committed to working together on the teams you're on and in the departments you join. The first step is commitment to the overall job or company, but you also have to commit to working together with your coworkers, who are part of your business—or to your spouse, who's part of your marriage; or to your teammates, who are part of your sports team; or to your other brothers and sisters in the church.

Working together isn't always easy. You can't just be committed to being on the team—you have to be committed to working together *as* a team.

Reading this book, implementing these ideas, and putting the Five C's into action lets you do that training before the game, so you're not left trying to figure it out in the moment, in the midst of confusion and conflict.

With this training, with this teamwork, we're all committed to working together and then we can improve the collaboration as a whole.

COMMITTING TO COMMITMENT

Before I met and married my current wife, I had another marriage end in failure.

I was younger, and I wasn't yet part of the church, so at the time I wasn't living up to the standards set forth in the Bible. Most importantly, I wasn't as committed as I should have been to making it work regardless of the circumstances.

But what about those times when it no longer makes sense to keep your commitment?

If you are in an abusive relationship, for example, you made a commitment to that marriage—but now it no longer makes sense to stay in that relationship. When you find out that the other party isn't committed to being in the loving relationship you initially committed to, that may be the time for you to do something different—whether that means a separation, extensive counseling, or as a last resort, divorce.

And this isn't only true in romantic relationships. You may have committed to a new job and then find that it puts you in a bad position—for example, that the company discriminates against women or minorities and has a very low glass ceiling. That wasn't your understanding when you took the job. When you joined the organization, you thought everybody was on a level playing field, but when you got there, you found out that what you were told is not reality. You committed to a job or a company that you understood to be a certain way. If that turns out not to be the case, you don't have to remain committed to that position under *any* circumstances, no matter what.

When I flew combat missions, I committed to go to that target regardless of whether someone was shooting at me or not—but I knew that was a possibility before I made my commitment. When someone discriminates against you or abuses you, you have to do something different to change your situation. That's not a lack of commitment—it just means that you have a greater commitment, to yourself and your health, safety, and ultimate success.

In 1984, a few years after the end of that first marriage, my wife, Shirley, and I got married, and we are all-in on making it work in the good times and the bad. When things are bad, we figure out how to fix it because we promised not to say, "I'm out of here." For us, divorce is not a viable option.

It's much easier to say "I do" when you get married than it is to actually *do* it in marriage.

We treat commitment as though our lives depend on it, and we have an exceptional relationship, but that has required a lot of teamwork.

Between the two of us, we have three sons, all from previous marriages. Two of our sons are very close in age—within a year—and the oldest of the three went through a rebellious phase in his teenage years. But we raised them, often without the benefit of their other biological parent, and we sent them all to college. We were very fortunate.

But one of the best things we did was treat them all the same and not make a distinction between them. They are not "your sons" and "my sons." They are all simply *our* sons.

Blending this family was one of the first areas in which my wife and I had to collaborate, and it required a lot of commitment—not just commitment to each other, but commitment to our family and how we chose to parent these children. Ultimately our commitment was to adhere to a biblical standard.

We didn't have a cookbook telling us what steps to follow to create this blended family. Children don't come with an instruction manual. What we did have were solid examples of this commitment to parenting in action.

My wife grew up as the oldest of the five kids her mother and father had together. Her father's first wife had died and left him with five children. He then married my wife's mother, and they went on to have five more children. My wife's mother treated all ten children as if they were her biological children.

I was also the oldest in my family, but I didn't really get to know my biological father until later in his life, shortly before he died. When I talk about my father—his work ethic, all the things we did together, the man I pattern myself after—I'm not talking about my biological father; I'm talking about the father who raised me. We may have had different last names, but he was my father. He never treated me any differently than his other three children. In fact, when my brother and sisters read this, they might say, "He treated you better!"

My wife and I never had a conversation about how to blend our families, but we both had excellent illustrations. And if we had not been all in—committed to God, to each other, and to our family—it would not have happened the way it did.

It's a lot easier said than done—and we did not do it

perfectly by any means—but when hers and mine came together to become *ours*, it was the most beautiful collaboration I've ever been a part of.

Commitment is the first step to better collaboration…but there are four more. The way ahead may still seem hazy, so it's time to get clarity.

EXERCISE

Are you most committed to team success or personal success? What would teammates say about you, based on your past behavior?

What does your effort look like when you're committed? How does it differ if you are not committed?

How do you know if your teammates are committed? What does their effort look like?

CHAPTER 3

═══

THE SECOND C: CLARITY

In Lewis Carroll's *Alice in Wonderland*, the Cheshire Cat asks Alice, "Where are you going?"

Alice responds, "Which way should I go?"

"That depends on where you're going," the Cat responds.

"I don't know," says Alice.

"Then it doesn't matter which way you go."

LET'S BE CLEAR

If collaboration is about moving together, clarity lets you see what direction you're going. Clarity means that something is easy to understand and execute, and it answers the questions, "Why?" "What am I doing?" And, "Where am I trying to go?"

Without these answers, people don't know what they're supposed to do. They don't know what the other people they are working with are supposed to do, either. And they don't have an agreement on what they're trying to accomplish. Ultimately, without clarity, a collaboration will fail.

In 2003, LeBron James left Cleveland and went to play with Dwayne Wade and Chris Bosh in Miami. They were three of the best players in the world—three future hall-of-fame players, one of whom had already won an NBA championship—on a world-class team. But you know what happened the first year they played together? They didn't win the championship. They lost to the Dallas Mavericks, because they hadn't yet learned to work together successfully.

One of the reasons the Warriors are so good historically is because they play a team game. People make sacrifices. Steph Curry could be the leading scorer in the league most years, but when Kevin Durant came, he stepped back. And they won two out of three championships because they played *together*.

But you can't just throw people together—even when they're superstar athletes—and think that they can just instantaneously work together and be the best at what they do.

To have a strong collaboration, there are three areas where we need clarity: communication, roles, and mission. If we're not clear in our communication, it increases the chance for errors and mistakes. If we don't have clarity around roles, it's hard to tell what's your job and what's my job. And if the mission itself is unclear, no one will know what the whole team is trying to accomplish, which makes it unlikely to actually happen.

But when you have clarity around all three pieces—when you're clear on your communication, when everybody is clear on their role, and when you're all clear on where you're going and how you're working together—you can be the best you're capable of being. Clarity promotes consensus and agreement because you're clear about expectations, so you know you're on the same page.

When you can see clearly, you know that you and the people you're collaborating with are going in the same direction at the same time.

Whether you're on a business team, a sports team, or in a marriage or other personal relationship, clarity of mission, roles, and communication allows you to maximize the potential of your collaboration.

MISSION

The first piece of clarity is getting clear on what the overall mission is. You have to be clear on the mission before you can break down the roles. Once you know what each person's role is, you have to communicate clearly so that you're all functioning within that mission. Everybody needs to be going in the same direction, working toward the same goal, but you can't do that without clarity.

When I was in the military flying combat, the mission was incredibly clear: the targets were A, B, and C. They gave us the coordinates and told us, "This is a search of an air missile site." I knew that we were flying reconnaissance, taking pictures of target sites.

K and I had different roles, not a different goal—and we put the goal before the role. The mission came first, before the individual's success.

In football, everybody is playing the same game, but their responsibilities are different.

If you're not clear on the overall mission at work—not just your role in it—it can lead to wasted effort, wasted dollars, and time spent that doesn't contribute to the bottom line. It may even make it more difficult for you and your team to work together.

If you're not a clear communicator, if you're not clear about your role, and *especially* if you're not clear about the overall mission, you're not likely to do well in your job. You're not likely to get promoted. And you're not going to be the person your team looks at to solve problems. You're going to have a real problem, particularly in a corporate environment, if the clarity isn't there.

BEST PRACTICES FOR MISSION CLARITY

Just like you want to document important aspects of your communication around your role, you'll want to document your mission or goal as well.

In a business environment, this may be your vision, values, and mission statement. This has to be agreed upon from the top, documented, and disseminated to the end users, the people on the team, so they understand what they're supposed to do as part of where you're all trying to go. That way, you and your entire team know that you have the same mission—and you have the same understanding of what that mission is.

If you're not fully clear on what the mission is, for any reason—whether you are the leader or a team member following someone else's lead—follow up and ask for clarification.

One way to make sure that you or your business is clear on the mission, once you've set a goal, is to measure how well you're accomplishing what you set out to do. Without clarity of mission, you won't make it—you won't know where you're going, so you won't know when you get there.

MISSION ACCOMPLISHED

Metrics are useful for determining how well you're doing with both short-term and long-term missions. You can look at the overall goal of what your company does or is aiming to do as well as a smaller, more specific mission of what you need to accomplish today—and then you can make sure that what you're accomplishing personally or in a smaller team fits in with the overall mission of the company.

Your daily or short-term mission will change a lot more frequently than the overall mission, so just like with clarity of communication and roles, you have to evaluate it on a regular basis. Our mission in Vietnam was always flying reconnaissance, but the specific targets changed daily. Your company may be developing a new product. Next year, once that product goes to market, you might be working on something else—your short-term mission changed, but the overall mission of the company didn't.

ROLES

Once you're clear on your mission, you also want to be clear on roles—both your role and the roles of other people you're collaborating with.

First, this allows you to make sure that you have complementary roles, that you're not both doing the same thing and duplicating your labor or leaving something undone. Clearly defined roles also allow you to maximize teamwork, so you don't have wasted effort. I'm not trying to do your job, and you're not trying to do mine.

When I flew those missions for the Air Force, the pilot in the front seat was called the aircraft commander because he had ultimate control of the aircraft. He was responsible for flying combat at low levels at night, and I was responsible for operating the cameras, navigating around the obstacles in front of us, and getting us over the target at a precise time.

But even though there was a hierarchy, and he was the aircraft commander, K never treated me like a second-class citizen. Neither of the two guys I primarily flew with in Vietnam—K and Ed—treated me like they were better than me; we just had different roles.

When you have clarity of roles and each person is performing to the best of their ability, your collaboration operates like a well-oiled machine. You are efficient. There's no debate about who is supposed to do what—you work together as a team.

It works that way in a marriage, too. You have to work together. If you're raising three kids with your partner, it's not just about what one person wants. You have to have the same financial goals, or goals about where you live or what kind of schools the kids go to, and you each have your part to contribute to that. For example, I work from home more than my wife, so I have more flexibility and freedom with my schedule. Because of this, I run most of the errands we need to have done, whether that's taking the clothes to the cleaners or picking up groceries for dinner. I told you earlier that she takes care of the finances; that's part of her role. That's the way we do it, to optimize our relationship.

If one person feels that the roles aren't clear, or if they feel that the other person isn't performing their role correctly, it creates friction, chaos, and confusion. But when you communicate clearly, and you revisit your discussion of roles and responsibilities, with the understanding that those roles can change, your relationship works better, too.

When you have clarity on roles—when you know that the other person understands their job and you understand yours—it leads to having confidence in yourself and that other person, which we'll talk about more in the next chapter.

BEST PRACTICES FOR CLARITY AROUND ROLES

To have a fuller understanding of the roles in your business, you may need to cross-train, or have an understanding of somebody else's role as well.

When my son started in the packaging and distribution business, he didn't know the business well—he had come from the banking industry. So he started on the assembly line, with the workers, so he could understand how difficult that job was and have a clear understanding of what the employees do on a daily basis. He didn't just need to learn how to manage; he needed a different viewpoint to get the whole picture.

He is now vice president of marketing and will become president of one of my companies in the next couple of years, when I retire. His son, who is a West Point graduate and is on active duty with the army, is getting out soon and will ultimately become president of my other company, but he will start out just like his dad started out.

Or, to use an example closer to home, if my wife got sick, I know how to do everything in our house as well. I may not do it all the time, but I know how to iron. I can pay bills. I know how to clean the floor, wash the windows, cook dinner—whatever there is to be done, we both know how to do it, because it's important to understand each other's roles and have some understanding of how to do them.

Finally, when Russ (the guy that I ejected with) and I flew in really bad weather, often in England, we couldn't see very well. In those cases, I could fly the approach using all the instruments from the back seat—and all he would have to do is look for the runway. That was a reversal of roles—he usually flew the airplane and I navigated—but he trusted me to fly the airplane well enough to fly the approach, and we both knew that he had the better view to see the runway because he was in front. Then, once we got low enough, and he spotted the runway, he would take back the stick and land the aircraft.

This tactic served another crew well when the pilot got shot in Vietnam. The navigator was able to fly the plane until right over the approach, and then the pilot was able to land the plane safely.

HOPE IS NOT A SOLUTION

Sit down and talk with the other people in your organization or on your team. Get on the same page. There is no miracle solution or a complicated process here. And hope is not a solution for a clarification of roles. You can't say, "This isn't working, but I hope it gets better."

You simply have to have a conversation. Review your handbook or documentation that we talked about in the previous section. Talk to your manager and the rest of your team—that's how you get clarity.

A lot of companies do an annual performance evaluation. If you don't have a good manager, you can be shocked at what you hear—because there wasn't clear communication. The role wasn't clear. You and the boss weren't on the same page about what you should be doing or how to do it. And if you wait a whole year to talk about it, it's even more of a surprise.

So you can't wait twelve months. Sometimes you have to manage your manager. If they don't initiate sitting down to talk about how you're doing, then you have to ask. If you disagree about something in the first quarter, you still have three more quarters to adjust. But if you wait until the eleventh month, you're up the creek without a paddle.

And if *you* are the manager, now you know how important it is to have clarity, so you can check in with your team to make sure they understand their roles while there's still time to make any necessary corrections.

COMMUNICATION

Clarity of communication doesn't mean being the one who speaks the clearest—or the loudest. It's not simply being clear about what you say but *how* you say it and the language you use.

On any team, it's important that participants all have the same definition of key terms and are on the same page.

IN MARRIAGE

For a period of time when our kids were in school, we lived in New Jersey, and my wife worked in New York City—with more than an hour's commute. At that time, I worked ten minutes from home. Guess who got to cook dinner and go to the kids' sporting events during the week? That's right, I did.

We had to be clear on how we were going to operate. There was no talk of what is "man's work" or "woman's work." If I had expected her to commute for over an hour, come home, and start making dinner, that would not have been reasonable or what's best for the team, which was my wife and I and the kids. We would have been a hungry team!

Shirley didn't have to tell me to cook—I just did it. I don't cook as well as she does, but it's edible. And my kids appreciated it—my wife did too, and that's good for the team.

IN SPORTS

Communication in sports may not be clear to people who are unfamiliar with the games, but the coaches and players certainly need clarity to be successful.

In professional football, for example, the coach calls a play, telling the linemen how to block, the running back whether or not he's getting the ball, the receiver which route to run, and so forth. Then the players get to the line and the quarterback, depending on the defense, might change the play. If the communication isn't clear every step of the way, it can lead to missed catches or interceptions.

Sports teams have their own forms of communication, too. Somebody sitting down to watch a baseball game for the first time may not know what an RBI refers to, whereas for an avid fan, that term is part of the game. Additionally, pitchers and catchers use hand signals to call pitches in baseball. They try to camouflage their intent from the opposing team, so the communication is clear only to them.

IN THE MILITARY AND MINISTRY

The military is yet another example of communication that may not make sense to an outsider but which is designed to be easily understood by the people involved in the collaboration.

When flying an airplane—whether civilian or military—certain jargon is used and understood by both the person speaking and the person listening. When the agency that's controlling the flight says, "Turn left to 2-7-0, start a descent from 5,000 feet to 2,000 feet," and a pilot says, "Wilco," both people must understand what that means: will comply. But someone who'd never been in an airplane would think, "What's wilco?"

K and I used the terms GCA, IFR, VFR, TACAN, WSO, GIB, AC, HF, FAC, DCM, and ACT—and anyone who flew the same missions as us knew exactly what those acronyms meant. If I use the same terms in civilian life, however, people don't understand what I'm talking about. They might think AC means air conditioning when, in this situation, it stands for aircraft commander.

As another example of a different kind of clear communication, when two planes fly in formation, they take off together but the pilot of the first airplane might not talk during the start of the takeoff. Instead, he leans his head back and taps on his helmet three times, indicating that he's ready to go. Then, as he starts pushing up the throttle with one hand and holding the stick with the other, he bows his head forward quickly so it's obvious that he's starting to take off.

When we were flying, even if the communication system

was out, we could still communicate. If I was flying and the person in front wanted to take control of the airplane, he would just shake the stick. That would indicate to me, in the back, "I want the airplane," and I'd take my hands off the controls.

Any of these ways of communicating may not be clear to the casual observer, but to the people involved in the communication, they are accurate and easily understood.

Clarity of communication aids in things being done the right way, while the reverse is also true: it's hard to perform to our maximum when we don't have good communication. If workers in a shop don't receive clear communication, they are likely to build the wrong thing. Unclear language can lead to confusion, doing things the wrong way, and wasting time and money. I've seen workers think they understand what they were asked to do, go out and do it, then bring it back only to be told, "That's not what I wanted."

If you can't clearly communicate what you want in a collaboration, whether as the leader or as a member of the team, you're going to have more failures than successes.

I was giving a sermon not too long ago, and I asked my congregation, "What is the purpose of the church?"

I heard a bunch of different answers: "It's the wish of God,"

"Fellowship," and so on. But according to the Bible, in Matthew 28, the main purpose is "to make disciples who make disciples."

My responsibility, from a leadership viewpoint, is not to make up my own definition but to define from the Bible what the purpose of the church is—and that's your leadership responsibility, in the important areas of collaboration for you. Ask several people the same question about a goal or the definition of a term, and you are likely to get many different answers. When the definition, goal, or desired outcome is clear and documented, however, people will be on the same page. But it's hard to be on the same page, if there is no page!

BEST PRACTICES FOR CLEARER COMMUNICATION

In the book *Language and Thought in Action*, the author, S. I. Hayakawa, puts forth the premise that the responsibility for communicating lies with the communicator. In other words, I have to take responsibility for communicating clearly and accurately to you—instead of making it your responsibility to try to figure out how to understand me.

One way to do this is to make sure we're both using the same language. Agree on the definitions of the words you're using. If you say "Wilco," make sure it means the same thing to the person you're communicating with.

Make sure that critical information is documented, that it's written clearly, so there's no misunderstanding and it can be referred back to. In a business environment, most people have visions, values, and mission statements written out in really neat ways—but those statements are more for other people. Internal communication needs to be clear as well, and it should also be reviewed on a regular basis so that it's familiar and easily remembered.

In the military, we were briefed before every mission—not necessarily on the planning of the actual mission, which we did individually or as a crew. Instead, that briefing was about anything else we need to be clear on *before* we planned and flew our missions—the weather, problems with the airplane, things that may need to be repaired. This consistent, clear communication allowed us to have greater success in working together toward the goals of our mission.

LET'S RAP

After flying our missions, I left Thailand before K did, but he and I ended up on the same base in England, though we no longer flew together.

The vice wing commander—the number two guy on the base—asked us if we would start a Wing RAPPER program: getting together with enlisted personnel, talking to them, and listening to complaints they had or areas where they'd like to see improvements. K and I would lead the discussion and then bring the men's concerns back to the vice wing commander. We each eventually earned the Meritorious Service Medal for this program.

But before that, when the vice wing commander first asked us to do this, I said to K, "You can be the chairman, and I'll be the vice chairman."

He was the aircraft commander, after all, and in the military, he ranked higher than I did.

"No," K said, "we're going to be co-chairmen."

This program had nothing to do with flying, and when we were out of the airplane, we were going to be equals—that's how much he respected my abilities. To him, it was never—in or out of the plane—that I had to do what he told me just because of his rank or because he'd been in the service a year longer than I had. No, he acknowledged that we had different roles, and he was the best at doing his—and he expected me to do my best at mine.

That clarity led us to have confidence in each other.

Similarly, your way ahead is clear, but you must step confidently into collaboration.

EXERCISE

Can the members of your team(s) accurately, clearly, and concisely verbalize the team mission and goals, as well as their individual responsibilities on the team?

Write them out for yourself. At your next team gathering, give each team member a blank sheet of paper and have each do as you have already done. Compare, discuss any differences, and determine why those differences exist.

CHAPTER 4

THE THIRD C: CONFIDENCE

Charlie Plumb was a captain who flew missions over Vietnam in a fighter jet. On his seventy-fifth mission—just five days before the end of his tour—Plumb was shot down over Hanoi. He had to eject, and he was captured and held prisoner for almost six years.

Years after his release, he was eating dinner in a restaurant when a guy walks up to his table and asks, "Aren't you Charles Plumb?"

Plumb doesn't recognize the man, but he says, "Yes, I am. And who are you?"

"I'm the person who packed your parachute."

They had never met before—Plumb didn't even know the person he'd put his ultimate confidence in—but that collaboration was part of the reason he was still alive. Maybe I should have called this book *Collaborate As If* Someone Else's *Life Depends On It*!

COMMITMENT AND CLARITY LEAD TO CONFIDENCE

Confidence is the feeling or belief that one can trust in or rely on someone or something.

We have confidence every day, without thinking about it: When we sit in a chair, we're confident that it's going to hold us up. When we drive across a bridge over a river, most of us don't hesitate because we have confidence that the bridge is going to hold the car. If you pay life insurance every month, you have confidence that it's going to pay off when you die—and you won't even be here to see it. When you work for somebody else, you work all week, or two weeks, or a month, and you don't get paid in advance—you have confidence that your employer is going to pay you.

Confidence grows as a result of commitment and clarity—said another way, commitment and clarity lead to confidence.

When you've trained and prepared, which we talked about

in the chapter on Commitment, and you're clear on your role and responsibilities, which we talked about in the previous chapter, you gain self-confidence and know that you can accomplish your goal. When teammates are trained and prepared, there is mutual confidence. This is what made me and K so good at what we did while flying combat.

If you're not committed, not trained, and not clear on your objective, you won't have the confidence you need to do what you're supposed to. As Henry Ford said, "Whether you think you can or think you can't, you're right."

Confidence may grow as you gain more experience—if you fly one mission and everything goes right and works well, by the third or fourth mission, you'll think, "We got this down."

The first time we go to do something, we're not very confident at all. You may think, "What if I mess up?" Even the first few times, you might wonder, "Am I doing this right?" Or, "Yeah, I've done it in training, but what's it going to look like in real life?"

On my first combat training mission, I got completely sick. It was hot, and I wasn't used to flying in an airplane at high temperatures, with limited air conditioning, and wearing a thirty-five-pound vest that secured my gun, spare bullets, and other items needed for survival in case I had to eject over enemy territory. The pilot said, "Doug, we're flying over North Vietnam," and I couldn't even look out the window because I was too busy throwing up.

But eventually, I got used to it. I adjusted, learned, and grew. Soon, I had confidence.

The more you fly, the more your self-confidence grows. The more you practice hitting or pitching, the more your confidence grows in your own skillset. When you first start a new job, you're not confident at all the first day. You don't know what you're doing, and you don't know the people you have to work with. But as you do the job, you learn and grow.

The more you collaborate, the more your confidence in yourself and your teammates increases—and the more confidence you have, the better you collaborate! They feed into each other and are reinforced as you have more success working together.

Confidence is not an event; it's something you get or have, and it can grow. Being successful on a continuous basis causes confidence to increase—but you still need the first two C's. You don't want to say, "Well, I'm confident now, so I can forget about my commitment or, I don't have to be clear."

You still have to work together.

ON SHAKY GROUND

If you lose confidence in someone—when your trust in them is shaken or broken—it makes your ability to collaborate much more difficult. You feel like you have to look over their shoulder to make sure they're doing what they're supposed to. You're concerned when they have to perform tasks you're not involved in—are they doing it correctly? Your workload increases. And not only are you doing work you shouldn't have to, but you're also carrying around this burden of heavy emotions—doubt, fear, and distrust.

John Whitney, a professor at the Columbia Business School, says that, "mistrust doubles the cost of doing business."

Remember that house we built in chapter 1, with commitment as the foundation, clarity and confidence as the walls, and caution and courage as the roof? Even if you have a solid foundation and a well-built roof, if you pull out one of the walls—if you lose your confidence—the whole thing is going to collapse.

CAUTION COURAGE CLARITY CONFIDENCE

COMMITMENT

On the flipside, however, when you do have confidence, it creates a bond among team members, which makes collaboration easier. It helps teams work together for the greater good.

Effective collaboration is not necessarily easy. You have to have confidence in the tools that you use, your skillset, and the ability to make decisions—your ability, as well as that of the person or people you're collaborating with.

TOOLS

First, you have to build confidence in the tools or equipment you use as part of your collaboration.

I don't care how good K and I were, if the camera systems didn't work, we didn't get the target—even if we did everything else exactly as planned. If the airplane didn't work, obviously that was a problem. An engine fire in the midst of combat over enemy territory? Even bigger problem.

K and I had confidence in each other—we were good at collaborating—but we also needed to have confidence in the equipment that was essential to the mission.

Maybe you're on a business team and you use a communication tool for your collaborative effort. You need to have confidence that the software is going to be reliable. You don't want to risk doing a bunch of work only to find out that you lost it. You need something that you know is going to work—whether that's software or hardware. When you don't have that, you're not going to be confident that you can fulfill the requirements of the job.

In a collaborative relationship, you need life tools: open communication and honesty. In a marriage, you have confidence that that person is going to be by your side every day. Your tools may be marriage counseling, books or courses, or even parts of the Bible that apply to how to treat other people.

More marriages fail because of money issues than anything else, so maybe you and your spouse take a course to learn how to get out of debt or read a book about investing or take a class to earn a new certification so you're not living paycheck to paycheck.

Using the best tools you have at your disposal gives you confidence that you are putting your best into and getting the most out of your relationship.

BEST PRACTICES FOR CONFIDENCE IN TOOLS AND EQUIPMENT

There's often some sort of tools or equipment you have to use at work, whether it's an airplane, a fire truck, a station on the assembly line, or a computer and related software.

If you're not sure which tools to use, it's relatively simple in this day and age to find the best one for the job. You can do a Google search and read articles and reviews. You can see what the manufacturer recommends or get a friend's opinion. That will give you some idea of how well it works, but ultimately you gain confidence by using it and seeing if it lives up to your expectations.

I'm sure my wife trusts me more today than she did when she first married me, because I have a nearly forty-year history of being trustworthy. Similarly, using a tool or piece of equipment with a proven history can also increase confidence. Using TurboTax's software to file taxes works because it's been around since the 1980s, even though it's changed a lot since then. As long as it's not something like a car, which eventually deteriorates with time, experiencing it and seeing that it does what it's supposed to do will increase your confidence in that tool.

Somebody also has to keep your equipment operating, doing the necessary maintenance on it or coming to fix it if something's wrong with it. You have confidence in the tool itself, but it can't fix itself, so you want to have confidence in the people maintaining or repairing it as well.

If you've ever worked in an organization where the computer support team is not very good, you know what I'm talking about. Your computer breaks, it takes a long time for someone to come take a look at it, and then the repair person tells you it's fixed…but it still doesn't connect. It's really disheartening—you can't get your job done because your computer doesn't work. You depend on the computer or the software to do your job, and when you can't use it, your confidence goes down the tubes.

Even when talking about tools or equipment, some of

your confidence comes from having confidence in other people's skillset—whether from getting a recommendation or trusting that the people who are supposed to maintain or update the equipment are doing their jobs.

When we flew our missions, we didn't fly the exact same airplane every time—but we did fly airplanes worked on by the same maintenance department. They kept those airplanes running, and told us when there were problems or when it was good to go. We had confidence in the airplanes because we had confidence in the people working on them.

SKILLS/SKILLSET

Next, you need to have confidence in your own set of skills. Having confidence in your own ability is what allows you to contribute to the success of the team.

The second day I was in Vietnam, I walked by the tennis court on my way to the mess hall and saw a man leading a karate class. I had always wanted to learn karate, but I never had the time, money, or a place to learn. This man taught a Korean style called Tae Kwon Do, and he gave lessons on the base.

When I started, I didn't have good flexibility. I could barely lift my leg waist high, and everybody else could kick higher than me. But I was told that if I practiced every day, there was a possibility of earning a black belt in a year. So, I went to class six days a week, and I practiced on my own on the seventh day.

When I earned my yellow belt, it gave me a little bit of confidence—and a new set of skills to learn. Then I passed another test, got a green belt, and became more confident still. Blue belt, brown belt—more and more confidence.

A year later, I took the final test—the black belt test—and I was the only one who made black belt from the class of people who had started with me. By that time, I could kick over my head and jump up to break boards held eight feet in the air.

After I left the military, I owned a couple of karate schools, and I taught my students the same way I was taught: how to hold their fists, how to punch, how to stand, how to kick. I'd have them practice the same moves over and over again—just like Mr. Miyagi in *The Karate Kid*.

They'd do the same simple movements again and again, until they became automatic. That way, when it came time for them to use those skills, they were there. You don't have time to think, "Hmm, he's punching at me with his right hand. I have to take my left hand and do an inside-out block now. I've got to twist my hips and counterpunch with my right hand."

You have to just do it! It becomes a conditioned response.

When you have confidence, you get to the point where you know what to do and it's automatic. You don't have to think about what to do or remind yourself to be confident. Instead, that confidence becomes part of you. And that confidence comes as a result of what you've already built—that decision to commit that you've made and the preparation and training you've done as a result, the clarity you've gotten around your mission, your role, and how you communicate. Now, you build on that until you get to the point where you feel confident without consciously thinking about it.

When Steph Curry shoots a three-pointer, often he doesn't even look to see if the ball went in; he knows it did. He sometimes looks to the other team's bench, to taunt them, then goes back down the court. When Klay Thompson shoots a three-pointer, a teammate often raises three fingers to indicate three points, and Klay heads back down the court before the ball even reaches the goal. Other guys on the Warriors see Steph or Klay shoot and, rather than going for the rebound, they just head back down the court too.

That confidence comes from having practiced making

those shots so many times that they *know* they're going to make it. They can feel it.

When you've seen the ball go through the basket, even just one time, your confidence level skyrockets—even on my level.

TRUST IN YOURSELF—AND OTHERS

Having confidence in your own skillset is just the first step. When you trust that the other person is as good at his job as you are at yours, you begin working together better.

When K and I were given a mission after we were already airborne, we had to figure it out literally on the fly. We didn't have the luxury of planning it out ahead of time. K couldn't look at the map and ask me any questions he may have had. Instead, we both had to rely on our tools, skillsets, and decision-making abilities.

I don't know if you've ever seen the inside of a fighter jet, but there's no room in the cockpit. If I put my elbows up, they'd hit either side of the cockpit. We couldn't stand up or even move around very much, and I had to unfold a map and try to figure out where we're going while K flew in circles at high altitude. We were given a bunch of coordinates, in code because it was over the radio, and my job was to figure out where to go. My tools were a map and pencil, a circular slide rule, a protractor and a compass—as well as the aircraft itself and the camera systems.

K and I had to rely on our own skillsets, but also on each other. When I told him where to go, he had to fly a mission for which he'd never seen the plans—he was completely dependent on my skillset. He had to have confidence that I had deciphered that code correctly, that I had plotted the coordinates correctly on the map, and that I could navigate us to that target—all with the added risks of getting shot at or running into a mountain or crashing. And I had to have complete confidence in his skills as a pilot.

When you and your team are confident that everybody is doing their best, the power of your skills isn't just added together—it's multiplied.

ABILITY TO MAKE DECISIONS

Confidence prepares us for the pressure we face, whether that's in combat, in business, or in life.

If you only have the skillset but you make poor decisions, you still have a problem. Your confidence can't just be in the skills; you have to know that you and your teammates are going to use those skills in the right way and at the right time, even under pressure. If you are flying combat and your airplane gets shot in the gas tank and you're running out of fuel, you want to be confident that you and the pilot are both going to do exactly what you're supposed to.

Once you see that happen, you begin to have some confidence, both in yourself and in the other person or people you're collaborating with. Then, when you get one win, your confidence increases—and you can build on that.

The first time I flew combat at night under these adverse conditions, in the dark with people shooting at us, I knew I'd been training and I had to have confidence in that—but I was committed to going out, making it work, and coming back. I didn't know for sure that I could actually do this until I went out and did it. And then I gained confidence by having lived through it.

After I'd been flying those missions for a while, even though I knew it was dangerous and that I could die if somebody shot us down, I had a lot more confidence in my ability. When we first started out, we thought we knew what we were doing—but we couldn't really know until we just did it.

BEST PRACTICES FOR BUILDING CONFIDENCE IN DECISION-MAKING ABILITIES

One of the best ways to build confidence in your or your

team members' ability to make decisions is by learning through failure.

We've established that repetition leads to confidence when you have repeated success, but failure has value as well. Life isn't going to be all success all the time. You're always hoping for success—you're not hoping to fail—but failure can be one of the best teachers, especially if you learn how to fail forward.

We practiced in a simulator before flying our missions, and we failed in that simulator so we didn't have to fail in real life. But I've failed in real life, too. When I got out of the military, I started a karate school. I found a nice place in a great location, made sure it was clean and attractive, and hired third- and fourth-degree black belts from Vietnam to teach the students. At the time, learning karate was extremely popular due to the popularity of Bruce Lee movies and the TV series *Kung Fu*.

And then Bruce Lee died and *Kung Fu* went off the air. The demand for learning karate declined, and as a result, we didn't have enough membership to sustain the studio. I learned from that—I had done everything right…except asking myself what I would do if something happened to Bruce Lee or if the *Kung Fu* series went off the air. How would I be able to market myself well enough to stay in business?

As a result of that experience—and the valuable lesson I learned—in future entrepreneurial endeavors, I have made sure to go through a process of looking forward and asking what can go wrong, how we can prevent it, and what we would do if that happens.

Failing does not make one a failure. We all make mistakes. As long as we're not continually making the same mistake, and we are willing to learn from it and utilize it to do better in the future, we can benefit from those setbacks.

Many Silicon Valley unicorns—meaning a tech startup with a market value of 1 billion dollars, like Twitter—didn't start out to be what they are now. They tried to be something else and were fortunate to pivot in a different direction. Some companies have some success and then aren't adaptable, and that leads to failure, but others are able to see that they can have more success if they grow and change. Those successful companies make a commitment to trying something, they get clear on the mission for one iteration, and then they go out and do it. Either they have some success, or they make a mistake, learn from it, and course correct. This process gives them some confidence, so they can either do it again or see where they can take it to the next level.

The first time you do something, you may not feel that confident. But at the end of the day, sometimes you just have to make a decision or you fail by default. Once you've made that decision and see the result, you can evaluate where you had success and what you may want to do differently next time.

Similarly, once you've started learning how to collaborate—as you've already done!—you don't have to start over every time you have a new collaboration. You can take this learning with you and apply it to working together better in every area of your life.

PLAY BALL!

I grew up in the South, during the height of segregation. We lived in the suburban part of town, and there was a park near our house where teams from other neighborhoods would come to play sports. We had softball, football, and baseball leagues—like Little League, but for us it was called Midget, Junior, or Senior League.

Because our parents worked a lot, we didn't have adults around to coach our teams, but five of my friends and I got together in the summer to play baseball. Six people aren't enough for a complete baseball team, so three guys from the other side of town who didn't have a team played with us. Two of them were exceptional baseball players. My friend, Melvin, was always better than us at baseball—and just about any other sport we played, too.

Every summer there was a City Championship game played between the team from one part of town, near the projects, and the team who won our Senior League—and that summer, it was us. We were committed to winning that championship. And we were clear on what we wanted to do: we wanted to beat those guys from the other side of town so bad.

I was just about the worst player, so I ended up playing right field where not as many balls are hit. I batted near the end of the lineup. Melvin was the strongest player and the best hitter, so he batted cleanup. We made a proper lineup. We were clear about where everybody played. I wasn't jealous that Melvin batted fourth while I batted eighth or ninth; I knew he was a better player than I was, and I wanted to win. So did my teammates.

In the championship game, we were behind or tied up most of the game. Late in the game, Melvin came up to bat, and we all held our breath. He hit the ball so hard and so far it flew out of the park, across the street, and into the front yard of a local resident. I can still remember watching that ball sail over everybody's heads. I don't even remember the score anymore, but we won that game! We didn't get a trophy, but we had bragging rights: we were the city champions.

We were committed to winning. It was clear that that was

our mission, and we knew what everybody's role was. We were confident that if we did our best and played to our strengths, we could beat the other team.

More than that, though, we had confidence in three areas: we had confidence in our tools, in our skillsets, and in our ability to make decisions.

We didn't have a lot of equipment; we had gloves and bats. Not everybody had a different bat, but we made sure we had enough for everyone to use the kind of bat that they needed. I didn't want to use the heaviest bat, for example, because I wasn't strong enough to swing it effectively. Melvin and a couple of other players who could really hit the ball the farthest, they used the heavier bats.

We spent more money than we should have on gloves because we wanted to get the best ones, gloves like the Major League players used. My parents couldn't afford that kind of glove for me, but I talked my aunt into buying me one to play with. (It helped that she was my mother's only sister and I was her favorite!)

Knowing that we had the best equipment we could use—the best tools for the job at hand—gave us confidence when we were playing. I knew I wasn't going to miss a ball because my glove was falling apart. I may miss it because

I missed it, but we had the best equipment we could get our hands on.

We also had confidence because we were realistic about exactly how much each of us could handle. I knew that I had limited abilities, but I was confident that if I did as much as I could within those abilities, and did it well, that we would win. I knew that if I could walk and get on base—not get a hit—and one of the batters after me got a hit and drove me in, I could score a run. Instead of trying to hit a home run, I would try any way I could just to get on base. I'd make sure that my defense didn't cause us to give up a run; I wouldn't miss a ball that was hit right to me.

I had confidence not just in myself but also in the abilities of the other guys on my team. If you needed me to hit a home run, we had already lost—I don't think I ever hit a home run in organized ball. But I knew that Melvin and a couple of the other guys were going to hit the ball really well. I didn't have a strong arm for pitching, but we had three guys who were good pitchers, so I trusted them to do their best. All I had to do was what I could do.

And it was clear to all of us that Melvin was the best player. Not only could he hit and pitch well, he also knew the game of baseball the best. Since we didn't have many adults around, he also acted as the coach for our team. He would say, "Doug, this guy coming up to bat is left-handed and he hits a long ball, move back." If he waved his hand toward himself, I'd come in closer. He determined the lineup, and we trusted him to be in charge. I only had to do what I was asked to do because I had confidence in Melvin's decisions.

EXERCISE

Ask yourself, "Who do I trust most in the world? Who trusts me?"

Think about someone with whom you have mutual confidence. How does it feel? How well do you collaborate?

What if I ask you to think about a team member in whom you lack confidence? How does that feel, and how well do you collaborate? How do you feel when there's a lack of commitment and clarity by team members?

Confidence is key, but if you are overly confident, it can cause issues, so it's important to also be cautious. Chapter 5 is the fourth C: caution.

CHAPTER 5

===

THE FOURTH C: CAUTION

The American poet Max Ehrmann wrote something in his 1920 poem "Desiderata" that has always stayed with me:

> "Exercise caution in your business affairs, for the world is full of trickery. But let this not blind you to what virtue there is; many persons strive for high ideals, and everywhere life is full of heroism."

MINIMUM VISIBILITY

When I was stationed in England, I flew a training mission to Germany with my friend, Don Stewart, whom I called Stu—one of the best pilots I've ever flown with. He and K are the only two pilots I would request if, for some reason, I ever had to fly the nighttime combat reconnaissance mission again. K initially taught me to fly the airplane, but it was Stu who taught me to handle the plane like an instructor pilot.

That particular mission started like any other. We got a briefing, planned the mission, listened to the weather report, selected an alternate base for landing if the weather was bad, and went through our checklists. Everything looked good, so we flew from England over Holland and Belgium, then over Germany, where we went from high-level flying to low level. When we flew lower, we saw that the weather had changed—it was so awful that we couldn't fly the low-level mission we had intended to fly.

I thought, *That's okay. We'll just land at the designated base in Germany.*

But when we got on the radio to get cleared for landing, they didn't have minimum visibility. When flying, we needed 300 feet of visibility vertically and one mile horizontally—otherwise, we were not supposed to fly into a base because we wouldn't be able to see the runway until the last minute and we could miss the runway or crash.

Okay, I thought, *Well, we always have the alternate base.*

For every mission, we never took off before determining an alternate base to land at in case the weather was bad at the base we were trying to go to—for situations just like this. So we asked to be diverted to our alternate base, but the air traffic controller said it was also below our minimum visibility.

I began to get a little concerned, but we were in Europe—there are lots of bases, and we were still close to Belgium, close to Holland. So I got back on the radio and said, "Give me any base in Europe that has visibility of 300 feet and one mile."

The air traffic controller came back on and said, "We don't have any."

That presented a serious problem.

Stu and I calculated how much fuel we had left and realized that we didn't have enough to get back to the base in England. Now we had a big problem.

It turns out, there was one base in all of Europe that had 300 and one visibility, but it didn't normally accept high-performance jets for landing.

We flew an approach—we didn't land; we just looked at the runway. It had an incline in the middle of it, so when you came in, it looked like the runway disappeared. It also had a very steep glide angle for the approach, meaning the angle you have to fly in at, to land the plane. We had to see how it looked and make sure we could land because we didn't have prior familiarity with this base.

This was our only chance, and we would soon run out of fuel. That would guarantee that we crashed, whereas trying for this runway only meant that we were in for a potentially difficult approach and landing.

Ultimately, we made it—we flew back in and landed safely, and we had to stay in the area for about a week until the weather was clear enough to fly back to our base in England. But that just shows that you can do everything right and still have things go wrong.

PROCEED WITH CAUTION

Everything we did—from briefings to planning to checklists to having an alternate base to flying in for an approach before landing at an unfamiliar base—was done out of caution.

Caution means being careful to avoid potential problems or dangers where possible, to avoid mistakes. You've probably heard expressions about caution before: "proceed with caution," "err on the side of caution," "a word of caution," even the word "precaution."

Caution is essential for sustained collaboration. Without it, we will not be prepared to deal with the problems a team is sure to encounter. Those problems don't always mean danger—though they might in the military or other places where your life is on the line—but something *is* going to happen in your marriage, in your ministry, at work, or on a sports team. It's great to think that the good times will last, and I hope they do as long as possible. But inevitably some problem, danger, or situation is going to arise.

Let's look at some examples.

You could be a farmer in the US and not know the President was going to put tariffs on China, and then you have a field of soybeans just rotting away.

My favorite NBA team, the Golden State Warriors, lost a championship because Kevin Durant tore his Achilles tendon and Klay Thompson tore his ACL, so they couldn't play.

My wife, Shirley, found a lump in her breast, went to the doctor, and had a mammogram. The doctor said that they could wait and observe it for six months and that there was "probably" a 70 percent chance that it "might not" be anything. Shirley told him that's not even a good free-throw rate and insisted that they do a biopsy right away, where they found cancer—fortunately at stage zero because it was detected so early. She took radiation treatment and her cancer is in remission because she brought her sense of caution into her collaboration with the doctors regarding her health and care.

No matter where you are in life, you're either going into a storm, in the middle of a storm, or coming out of a storm—that's life. Without caution, you're unprepared to deal with those storms. The probability of making mistakes increases, and then confidence may decrease.

But when you have caution, you are able to think through the potential difficulties, dangers, or pitfalls down the line so you don't take unnecessary risks. You can figure out the desired end result and then work backwards to identify and plan for areas of concern.

Some people want to build a company with the end goal of selling it and cashing out. I built my companies to be something that will continue to provide income for me and my wife, that my son and grandson can take over, and that they can grow into something bigger that will continue to help the family and do some good for society.

If I were just trying to sell the company, I'd make one set of decisions: I'd look at the short term, trying to maximize profits so I could sell it for the highest amount. But because I want to build a company that is lasting and sustainable, I make a different set of decisions, looking to the long term and exercising caution to make sure my decision is in line with what we're trying to accomplish.

To use caution to your advantage, at home and at work, you can prevent problems before they occur (when possible), have plans for multiple potential outcomes, and rely on what you've learned from training and past experiences.

PREVENT PROBLEMS BEFORE THEY OCCUR

Whenever possible, you want to prevent problems *before* they occur.

If you have six people on your team at work and the CEO gives you a task to do, what happens if you can't agree? How will you resolve it if it's three votes to three?

Well, you can communicate with the CEO before you ever get to a stalemate, to know if you should bring it to him or her at that point, or if you should keep working until you figure it out. You can elect one person to guide the team and be the one who communicates with the CEO, to make sure there aren't six different people telling him or her six different things.

Addressing it ahead of time, not in the heat of the moment of disagreement, allows cooler heads to prevail. If it gets to the point of actively disagreeing, you're not going to agree on anybody being the leader. The CEO is going to get six angry people marching into his or her office saying, "Look at what this idiot said!"

The CEO is going to be angry that the team isn't working together well, and the team is going to suffer, too.

Rather than finding yourself in this predicament, do everything you can to anticipate problems before they become, well, a problem.

TAKE PRECAUTIONS

In the military, before we flew, we were briefed on the weather. We always had an alternate base we could land at, in case the weather got bad. We had checklists that I read out loud every time we flew—for take-off and landing, landing gear down, flaps up—and K responded, "Check," to make sure we didn't miss anything. We had other checklists that were there in case something went wrong—what to do if there was an engine fire, for example. They had predetermined the kinds of things that can happen and provided the sequence of steps to take should those things occur.

We had safety meetings, where we learned about other RF-4C airplanes that had crashed, what happened, and the results. We were tested on emergency procedures and watched training videos. Every year, even though we were trained well and did our jobs well, we had an annual check ride when an instructor flew with us on a mission, to ensure that we were proficient.

I never got into an airplane with the intention of ejecting, but every single time I got in, I put the straps around my legs that would draw my legs back in case I had to eject. I connected my risers to the seat with the parachute in it. I put on my seatbelt, hooked up my G-suit, and made sure I had on my oxygen mask. I checked to make sure the seat was on automatic, so I didn't have to do anything manually other than pull the ejection handle, if necessary. I did this every single time, because that was procedure—it was precautionary, in case something happened and the airplane was about to crash, but that precaution allowed us to work together better because we felt safe.

The military leadership had taken every precaution for what to do in an emergency—and K and I never had a disagreement about what to do or who would do what, because it was predetermined.

BEST PRACTICES FOR PREVENTING PROBLEMS

You can never completely eliminate risk, but you can minimize it by operating under the umbrella of caution. There's no magic wand, however—you have to do the work.

When I do premarital counseling, one of my objectives is to ensure that people don't wait until they've been married for a year and there's not enough money to pay the rent to figure out who's going to handle the finances or what sort of financial obligation each person has.

There may already be some problems before the wedding, and wedding planning is stressful, but right after getting married is the honeymoon period. Everything's great, and people think it's going to be easy and fun forever—then, bam! They find out the other person has a ton of debt, which now becomes their debt, and suddenly they're both in a precarious financial situation.

When you go to premarital counseling, you can prevent some problems before they occur, because you're relying on the wisdom and objectivity of somebody who has seen other people go through this, and who is trained in asking questions you may not have thought about. When I marry people, I always tell them, "Six months down the road, or whenever stuff happens that you can't handle, call me—I'm always available."

Although you can't predict the future, you can talk about aspects of your relationship to try to prevent possible problems before they occur. Do you plan to have kids? If so, are you both going to work after you have kids? If one person's job moves, how will you decide whether to stay or go?

People often don't talk about these things until they're hit in the face with it, but it can be helpful to know some of these answers ahead of time. When times are good—when you're headed toward that desired result—that's not the time to coast. You can't rely on those good times lasting forever, so that's the time to start considering what problems are coming and how to prevent them.

Precaution sets the ground for future collaborations as well. You're currently working to prevent problems in the present, but that can help prevent problems in the future as well, because you've thought them through and are taking steps to keep them from happening.

Collaboration is not a goal, it's a process—you can always continue to improve upon it. As successful as K and I were on the missions we flew in Vietnam, we never arrived to the epitome of collaboration. There were annual check rides, and we were continuously tested. We never got to the point where we didn't have to learn, get tested, or be evaluated anymore—and that's what helped keep us in top form.

HAVE PLANS FOR MULTIPLE POTENTIAL OUTCOMES

You can't always prevent problems from happening, but you can be prepared for them when they do occur.

Caution can be instrumental when working backwards from a desired end result, because it allows you to answer the question, "What could go wrong?"

When you have considered that question, it means you've thought about it, you're familiar with multiple possible outcomes, and you've had the opportunity to come up with plans, alternate plans, backup plans, and how you'll collaborate to solve those problems.

When I was a management consultant, I would divide the managers into two teams and give them each a hypothetical scenario that would be critical for the company. For example, "If the power went out and we couldn't operate, what would we do?"

Each team would devise a plan for what to do in that situation. Then we would get back together and look at each plan. We could use both plans or look at the best parts of each, but either way, we knew how to react if we ran into those difficulties.

Even though that situation may have never happened

before—and hopefully would never happen—we were prepared for how to survive that storm.

When we flew in Vietnam, our desired end result was to take pictures of the targets. One of the things that could go wrong, however, was getting shot at by the enemy.

The airplane we flew in, the RF-4C was originally designed as an F-4C, a fighter jet, but they took off the guns, bombs, and missiles and replaced them with cameras in the nose, to do reconnaissance on surface-to-air missile sites, bridges, troop movements, etc. The airplane looked like the fighter jet, but if we were shot at…we couldn't shoot back.

The solution? When we flew more dangerous missions, we had fighter escorts with us.

We often flew at low levels, close to the ground, and we flew pretty fast so we could get over the target, take the picture, and get out of there. Because we didn't have guns or missiles on our plane, when we flew low-level missions over North Vietnam, a couple of fighter jets that did have guns and missiles would fly with us. Then we could descend to low level and fly our mission. If somebody began to shoot at us, we could radio back to the fighters at high level and have them come fire on the target.

We had these fighter escorts collaborating with us out of

caution—we couldn't defend ourselves. We couldn't fight back, but they could.

BEST PRACTICES FOR CONTINGENCY PLANNING

You can do the same thing with your teams that I did with mine:

Whether as a group or in smaller teams, come up with hypothetical problems that could potentially apply to your situation. Are you at a danger for hurricanes, power outages, fires, or flooding?

Some industries can keep going if they lose power, but others would probably have to stop for the day. But do you just throw up your hands? Or is there a way to make it work?

If, for example, you've established a relationship with a company that provides mobile generators—*before* the storm hits—when you're in need, they can bring one in so you have power again.

What are some other possible solutions to the problems you may face? What happens if you aren't struck by that storm—but your supplier is? If they're your only supplier, and what they supply is critical to your finished product, what's your backup plan in an emergency situation?

You can't think of every situation that is ever going to happen, but you *can* consider some situations that are more likely to happen or that have happened before. Once you have a plan in place, you can modify or adapt it for other situations. Plus, you have the experience of thinking it all the way through from the situation to the desired result.

Remember, the time to think about these things is not after the storm hits and the power is already out.

RELY ON WHAT YOU'VE LEARNED FROM TRAINING AND PAST EXPERIENCE

Caution is looking at your desired end result and working backward to give you the best chance of achieving that goal, but you also need to have training and practice so that when you encounter those problems or get into those dangerous or stressful situations, it's not the first time you've worked through what you're supposed to do.

In the previous section, you thought through possible scenarios and outcomes. With training and practice, however, you've prepared how to react and respond in critical situations. You crash and burn in practice so you don't have to do it in real life.

In the military, we had lots of training and practice, but

one that prepared me the most for danger was the flight simulator.

Inside the flight simulator is everything the airplane has in it—controls, screens. If you turn left, the simulator moves left. If you turn right, or move up and down, it moves too.

The point of the simulator was to allow you to experience extreme situations without having to actually place you in danger. For example, it could simulate an engine flame out, and we would have to go through our checklists, figure out what to do, and demonstrate that we could recover the airplane.

When I had to eject in real life, I had done it many times before—in the simulator. I didn't have to think about how to get out—I didn't even have *time* to think—I just did what I had practiced. And if I hadn't been through the simulator all of those times, if I hadn't had this experience going through it to know what it looks and feels like, we both would have been dead. There's no way we could have successfully ejected without having trained properly in the simulator, where we could crash without consequences.

We crashed so many times in the simulator—again and again, until we got to the point where we could perfect what we were doing. That led to us having confidence that we could do it in real life because we had trained and done it wrong in the simulator until we could do it right.

BEST PRACTICES FOR BEST-LAID PLANS

It is possible to be too cautious and end up paralyzed in the planning, preparation, or training stage.

At some point, you just have to act.

Caution cannot be an excuse for cowardice. You've spent all your time developing and testing a product—you need to put it out there, get some feedback, and try to improve on it. If Apple had waited until they got to the iPhone 10 version to put it out, it would have been a much better phone than the first iPhone—but think how much money they would have lost.

In a collaboration, you are not operating alone. Turn to your partner, your company, or your friend—and just do it.

In the book *The Five Second Rule*, the author Mel Robbins watched NASA count down to firing a rocket and turned that into a concept for taking action. She advises people to literally count backwards from five and then on to "one," and then you do whatever it is you need to do.

You've done everything you can—you've committed to

training, you're clear on what you're doing, you've got confidence in what's going on, and you're ready to act.

You can also turn to your standards. We all need standards from which to operate. In the military, we had Air Force manuals, rules, regulations, and procedures—standards against which I could evaluate what I was and was not supposed to do. In church, our standard is the Bible.

Companies don't always have a standard. Maybe they have a mission statement, but it's just for show. If values aren't clear and published, it can be difficult to know what to do. When you go through this process with the Five C's, however, you end up with clarity about roles, responsibilities, and goals—so now you've created a standard about what you're trying to achieve and what each person is supposed to do as part of that.

That's why sports teams often have a mantra or slogan for the year. It's something they can build on, so they're all on the same page.

If you have a clear standard by which to measure yourself, your relationship, your team, or your company, it becomes easier to know what to do when everything goes wrong.

ACCORDING TO PLAN

No mission ever goes 100 percent according to plan. Dwight D. Eisenhower once said, "In planning for battle I have always found that plans are useless, but planning is indispensable."

When I planned our missions, I spent two or more hours with my maps and instruments, figuring out the degrees of bank and at what ground speed we would have to fly. I shaded in the map with what I anticipated seeing on the radar scope, based on the way the typical scope reacts to the land masses we flew over. It was as exact a science as I could make it, but nothing ever worked out exactly as it looked on those maps.

We would fly a little bit off course and have to make corrections. If we ran into clouds, we might have to change course entirely, just like when you make a business plan and run through projections, anticipated competition, and expected growth in the market—they're all the best of plans, but they're also based on the assumption that everything will go as planned.

Plan as if you are going to be 100 percent correct, but know in your heart that there will have to be course corrections along the way.

All of this caution strengthens the collaboration as a whole.

Then you've had the experience of preventing problems when you can, working through them when you can't prevent them, and thinking about how to handle them.

EXERCISE

As you start to make and implement plans with your team, ask yourself, "What's the worst that could happen if I do this? What's the best that could happen if I proceed?" Use your answers to optimize the course of action to be taken.

Caution will not eliminate danger, but it provides a plan for reacting to danger if and when it occurs. At some point, however, one simply has to go into battle. Caution is important, but you don't want to get stuck being *too* cautious—courage is necessary as well.

Once you've identified obstacles and created a plan to overcome them, you need courage to do something in spite of the fear of doing it.

CHAPTER 6

THE FIFTH C: COURAGE

There is a difference between courage and bravery.

If your neighbor has a "Beware of Dog" sign in his yard, bravery is going into their yard without fear.

Courage, however, is only going into that same yard if, for example, your child or grandchild has wandered over and is in danger—even, or especially, if you're afraid to do so.

FEATS OF COURAGE

Courage is the ability to act in the face of adversity, and it is an outgrowth of the other four C's. It's hard to have courage if you're not committed to, clear on, and confident about what you're doing. You can have caution and plan for potential pitfalls, but when you're facing disaster, you need the ability to demonstrate courage.

People often think that courage is something to just be conjured up in the moment, but courage is actually a culmination of what has already happened and what we've already learned. It can't be taught, but we learn from experience—and that's how we discover our courage, too. Often when we demonstrate courage, we don't have time to think, we just react, so these other things have to already be in place.

Having courage implies a willingness to sacrifice, whether life, limb, or well-being. It is the appropriate response to risk that has been minimized by caution. Courage is not the absence of fear, but rather responding appropriately in spite of fear—feeling fear, yet choosing to act and keeping on in the face of adversity.

And anyone can be courageous. Having courage is not limited to any race, gender, height, size, or education level. You may not even know that you have courage until you're in the midst of responding to an extreme, dangerous, or high-pressure situation, but we all have the potential to demonstrate courage.

If you've made it this far but you don't add this final piece— if your house of collaboration is built but the roof is only half finished—you're still not going to have a successful and sustained collaboration.

Again, no matter how well you plan anything, it's never going to go exactly as you planned it. In the words of Mike Tyson, "Everybody has a plan until they get punched in the face." The idea is to get as close to your original plan as you can, but you also need flexibility when things don't go according to that plan.

Without courage, you may hesitate to act, whether that's implementing a new policy, taking a product to market, or finalizing a cure for a disease. These delays can have a negative impact on your top line and bottom line because doing nothing—or delays in what you should do at the appropriate time—costs money. You have to have courage to act in spite of the potential for failure because, as we established in chapter 4, you can still learn and grow through failure.

This may sound contradictory, but you also need courage in order to *not* do things too—things you're not supposed to do. Part of courage is not doing the wrong things, in personal relationships, in ministry, or in corporate entities.

If we do make mistakes or do something wrong, we need to have the courage to own up to it and correct it as soon as possible. You have to look to the long term and do what's best for the team, for the collaboration, rather than what's best for you, the individual, in the short term.

If you have a car accident, you probably wouldn't hide it from your spouse and try to get the car fixed without letting the other person know about it. Instead, you would say something like, "I made a mistake, and it was my fault. I hit a pole, and I know we don't have much money, but I'm coming to you so we can figure out how to deal with it."

When my son was in college, I told him, "I know you're busy with school, so you don't have to go to church every Sunday, but I expect you to go twice a month."

At the end of a month, I called and asked him, "How was church?"

"Fine," he replied.

"Where'd you go?" I asked.

He told me, but I had a suspicion he wasn't telling me the truth, even though that wasn't like him.

"Okay," I said, "What did the preacher preach about?"

"Something from the Old Testament," he said vaguely.

So I asked, "What side of the church is the organ on?"

Finally, he admitted, "All right, Dad. I didn't go to church!"

He knew that I would have gone to that church just to see what side the organ is on—and he also knew that he hadn't done what he was supposed to do. He figured it was better to tell me he went even though he didn't so that I wouldn't harass him about not going.

In that moment, he didn't have the courage to tell me the truth—but that was when he was younger, and now he knows that even if I'm not going to like it, he can do the right thing so that I keep my trust in him.

The courage you need to have as a father is different from the courage you may need as a minister, as a husband, as a soldier in combat, or as a business owner.

You've already shown courage by reading this far, by being willing to admit that maybe you're not collaborating as well as you could be, and by taking the chance to pick up a book to learn how to collaborate better.

This chapter can't teach you how to have courage, because it can't be taught. But we can discuss how to recognize courage, when you might need it, and how to put yourself in the best position to utilize courage when confronting obstacles, frustrations, and fears.

OBSTACLES

If you have the Five C's in place, you are in a better place to be courageous. With courage, you see that an obstacle is just an opportunity to overcome, not something that stops you. You don't alter your course so much that you can't achieve your goal. Instead, you may pivot, you may change something, or maybe you make a course correction, but you don't see the obstacle as a stop sign—it's more of a caution sign.

My son, Geoff, went to a well-known prep school here in New Jersey. He was a good student and, at the beginning of his senior year, Geoff went to the counselor and told her where he wanted to go to college, which included the University of Virginia, Georgetown, Dartmouth, Stanford, Yale, and Princeton.

She looked him right in the eye and said, "Geoff, you're dreaming. You're not going to get into those schools."

He came home extremely disappointed. My wife and I didn't have any extra money then—we had another kid in prep school and one in college, and it was everything we could do to pay the tuitions. But Geoff was so disillusioned and down that my wife said, "I don't care how much the applications cost—you apply to the schools you want to go to, and we'll pay for it."

Geoff applied to those schools, and he was accepted everywhere except Stanford. Four years later, he graduated from Princeton—and his son went on to graduate from West Point.

When we encouraged him to apply (see that word, "encourage?" It has the word courage right in it), we put courage into him. And then he took that courage to go ahead and apply. But if he had listened to that counselor—if he hadn't been able to overcome that obstacle—he could have wasted his amazing potential.

In life, you are going to face obstacles. You are going to have to overcome adversity, whether it's internal, holding yourself back, or external, when somebody else tries to hold you back. If you have a startup or are trying to get a new product on the market, there are always going to be naysayers.

Having courage means taking into consideration appropriate criticism but in the end making your own decision about what the appropriate action is—and having the courage to do it in spite of the naysayers.

FRUSTRATIONS

Collaboration can be frustrating. A group of people with different backgrounds and experiences are thrown together and expected to make it work. And anytime you're dealing with people, you're going to experience frustration.

The way to deal with frustration is to expect it to happen. You anticipate that you will be frustrated—and so will other people. It's not an aberration; it comes with the territory, and you can't let frustrations stymie you or prevent you from achieving your goals.

If your teammate is acting up, you may not have anticipated that they would act in that way or that it would happen today—but you can expect frustrations as a part of doing business. And because you set those expectations, you're better able to deal with the frustration, and you have the courage to do so.

This is another one of those scenarios where if you can think about it ahead of time, you can ask yourself, "What can I do?"

Again, you may not be able to think of every situation in which somebody or something can be frustrating—and that wouldn't be a good use of your time—but you can think about what you can control and how you can react.

I've been married for more than thirty-five years, and I've

learned that my wife will occasionally suffer from some degree of depression and, when she does, her reactions to things are more extreme. That can be frustrating, but it's part of being married to and living with another person.

So on the infrequent occasions where it has happened—where she hollered at me or had an extreme reaction to something—I don't have to overreact to it. That would make it worse. I wait for the appropriate time and calmly ask, "Are you depressed?" and she might respond, "Yeah, maybe. I'm not feeling well today."

I don't let that threaten our marriage relationship, which is our collaboration. I know what's happening, I recognize what I can control—my reactions—and we can both move forward.

Of course, I learned this from experience. I made the wrong decision a few times, but I learned from those and reacted differently the next time. We're all learning all the time.

Once when I was still in the military, I was planning our next mission when my squadron commander came in and started getting on my case about something. We got into a verbal fight in the conference room, right in front of all the other aviators. I don't remember exactly what the issue was anymore, but I knew I was right and he was wrong.

Even so, I should have remembered that this was my commander. I was a captain, but he was a lieutenant colonel—my boss's boss. If I was still going to fight with him, we should have gone into his office and argued in private.

When it came time for evaluations, my commander marked me down one level below the highest level of evaluation, which I should have received. I should have exercised caution, taking into consideration who he was and where we were, not blowing up—even though I was right.

When you're frustrated with someone and you become so concerned with being right or proving your point, you can blow up the whole collaboration—that's definitely winning the battle but losing the war.

On a team or in a business group—even in a marriage or in the military—you have to pick your battles, choosing wisely about what you're willing to fight for. And particularly for those in charge, you have to allow everybody to be heard, to make their point, even if you do something different—and even if it's frustrating to do so. Simply trying to work together will make the relationship and the collaboration better.

FEARS

Without courage, you make decisions—or fail to make decisions, getting stuck and holding yourself back—from a place of fear. That fear is a normal emotion. It's our bodies' response to danger, and we need that. But when we let it control us, rather than responding to it appropriately, then we don't accomplish anything.

The motto of our reconnaissance mission was "alone, unarmed, and unafraid." When we thought about people shooting at us, trying to kill us, it put some fear in us—but we couldn't allow that to make us choose the wrong course or keep us from flying our mission.

In the business environment, you might be afraid of trying something that doesn't work, such as spending the company's money and seeing the stock go down. But you can't allow your fear to lead you to make the wrong decision or no decision at all.

As I've mentioned, courage is something you have, not something you learn. And that's why the Five C's are so important. If you're really committed and trained well, if the goals and roles are clear, if you are confident in the tools you use and the other people involved, if you've looked at the potential dangers or things that could go wrong and determined a course of action—if you've done the best you can do with the information available, then everything is in place for you to go forward and act with courage, secure in the knowledge that you've done everything you can to be as successful as possible.

People will always be afraid of something, but choosing to let go of or move past those fears is what finally allows you to be open to full collaboration. Don't let fear hold you back or you may miss out on something wonderful.

In the last chapter, we talked about having a contingency plan, thinking through a scenario before you're actually in it and fear or other emotions are riding high. When you plan ahead and even train for that situation—running emergency drills, for example—you're creating a degree of familiarity so it's not as scary if it does ever happen.

You can create checklists, at work and at home, for disaster preparedness—whether those are lists of things to have in case of an emergency or the steps of your plan in case the power goes out.

You can use the fourth C—caution—to make those plans so that in the fifth C here, in courage—you're not letting fear take the wheel. You feel the fear, but you choose to act anyway, letting your muscle memory, the checklist that you've memorized, or the plan that you've practiced, guide you through the situation.

As the late pastor Adrian Rogers once said, "Courage is fear that has said its prayers."

COLLABORATION UPON COLLABORATION

In a previous job, I was the management consultant for a packing and distribution company. I had a company called Recon Consulting, LLC, named after the reconnaissance missions I flew.

The packaging and distribution company was my only client, and my wife worked there as the director of finance and administration. I reported to the CEO who ran the packaging and distribution division. When people asked what I did, I said, "Anything the CEO doesn't want to do," whether that meant writing a bonus plan, chairing meetings, or anything else.

One day, he called me into his office upstairs and asked if I would be able to start a staffing company. He and his partners were trying to sell the company to a publicly traded company, and they wanted the warehouse employees off of their payroll so that the purchasing company wouldn't have to offer the warehouse employees benefits and retirement plans.

I said yes, thinking I could do it slowly, over a few months. But the partners wanted it done immediately, so within a few weeks, I set up the company, got some office space, and started with six hundred employees—with a contract saying I had exclusive rights to provide employees to the packaging and distribution company, even if it was later sold.

Unfortunately, the partners didn't end up selling to that company, and when the deal fell through, I still had my staffing company. When another larger company eventually purchased the packaging company, they brought in their own financial people, so my wife came to work with me.

She is a fantastic asset with a strong background. She's very skilled in finances and she's been working in the industry since the mid-1990s. But that also meant that we were always together, *everywhere*—at home, at work, at church, on vacation, and with the kids.

I like to think that she and I do it as well as any couple could. Overall, it works very well for us. We've grown the company from 600 to 3,600 employees. In 2015, we put together a joint venture with the company that acquired the old packaging company. The joint venture's major customer is a large pharmaceutical company, with whom I had worked when I was involved as a management consultant, setting up the major facility that we now operate for them.

In 2018, the joint venture won three awards, each nominated by the same pharmaceutical company: Minority Veteran's Business Enterprise of the Year, New York and New Jersey Minority Supplier Development Council Supplier of the Year, and National Minority Supplier Development Council Regional Supplier of the Year.

We also have a son who works with us. He's the VP of marketing for both companies, and my goal is for him to take over one of the companies when I retire. His son is a graduate of West Point and will be leaving the military soon, so he'll come and work with us also. I'll feel very blessed to eventually have four family members in my companies—and maybe at some point we'll have even more!

It's a different kind of collaboration than most companies have, because this collaboration represents not only our business but also our retirement, our future, and our legacy. We are very passionate about it, but it took a lot of courage to do what we've done.

I remember wondering, *What if it doesn't work? How could I fire my son? Or what if it works but not well enough and we need someone else to take over?*

But we turned to the Five C's. By putting the two companies together, we got the benefit and agility of a smaller corporation that can respond to our customers' needs but with the backing of a much larger corporation that's much better funded.

Once that commitment was there, we had to be clear on what our roles were, particularly as we obtained the various required certifications as a minority-owned business enterprise and a veteran-owned business.

We gained even more confidence after one employee, said, "We thought staffing was just staffing and we could hire anybody to do that!" Then they realized that we brought something that nobody else could bring.

We do have to have caution and be mindful that we can't be everything to everybody, that just because an opportunity comes up doesn't mean it's something we should do.

And again, it took courage to make this work to be beneficial to all of us—and it is.

EXERCISE

Who do you see as having demonstrated courage? Why do you feel the way you do about them?

My list of courageous men and women includes my fellow combat aviators because they were committed to putting their lives on the line; astronauts because they have to be tough to go through the training they do; missionaries who dedicate their lives to serving and helping others; firemen, policemen, 9/11 responders, and military heroes because they risk their lives every day; Martin Luther King, the Freedom Riders, and leaders of the Civil Rights Movement, because although we still have a ways to go, we've also come a long way in the relatively short period of time since then, and those people had to demonstrate courage. Many of them went to jail. Some were beaten and spit on. They risked their lives to improve the lives of those who came after them.

Now that you know the Five C's, let's bring it all together in your life.

CONCLUSION

When I went through flight training, the instructors showed us training films to help us determine what to do when the airplane goes into certain out-of-control situations. To make one such video, a crew intentionally put the airplane into a flat spin. The problem was, they couldn't recover the airplane from the spin, and it crashed.

The crew ejected safely, and they were able to recover the camera, so we were able to see that full recording as part of our training.

Three or four years after Vietnam, I was stationed in England and navigating on a normal training mission flying low level to take radar pictures of some targets in Holland. I was in the rear, reading the radar scope, and the young lieutenant pilot I was crewed with then, Russ, was flying the airplane.

Nothing out of the ordinary happened until we began to descend from high level to fly lower over some civilian targets as part of the training process. There were some clouds in front of us, so Russ asked, "Can I deviate around the clouds?"

"Yeah," I replied, "I'll get us back on course."

I knew there were some islands nearby, and those are easy landmarks to pick out on a radar scope.

As he began to fly around the islands, I looked up and saw what was going on outside of the cockpit. The airplane had gone into this wild gyration, pointing to the ground and then coming back upright. I thought to myself, *This is just like the movie.*

My first words to Russ were, "We're in a spin."

It was a flat spin, and the only other time I'd seen it had been in that training video, because pilots don't intentionally put the airplane into that situation.

The airplane was going around and around. If you take something flat, like a plate, and put it on your desk and move it around in a circle—that's a flat spin. We were going around 360 degrees, just spinning.

We had just checked our altimeters, which was normal procedure at 10,000 feet to make sure that the front and rear cockpit were both reading the same altitude. And we both knew that in this particular aircraft, if you were out of control below 10,000 feet, even if you got it back under control, you wouldn't have enough room to recover. That was critical.

After I said, "Russ, we're in a spin," he yelled, "Doug, we're below 10,000 feet, get out, eject, eject, eject!"

There was no further communication—and none was needed. In fact, I never even heard him say, "Eject." As soon as I recognized that we were in a spin below the minimum ejection altitude—and the plane was going down—I started the ejection sequence.

I don't remember very much from pulling the ejection handle until the opening shock of the parachute jolted me as it deployed. That let me know that the parachute worked. I don't remember the canopy being ejected, the rocket motor firing my seat from the aircraft, being detached from the seat, or the actual deployment of the parachute.

Russ remembered more than I do. He recalled the canopy going off, and he actually saw the airplane explode on the ground while he was still going up in the ejection seat. I do remember looking around for Russ, and I couldn't find him, but that's because I was about twice as high as he was. His parachute opened, it took one swing, he pushed off the side of a house, and then he hit the ground.

A few seconds later, and neither of us would have gotten out.

When I ejected, I was coming down over water. It was just a pond, but I couldn't tell how deep it was.

In that moment, however, I remembered everything from the sea survival school I had been through several years earlier. I knew, without really having to think about it, the sequence of things to do when you are over water—put my hand on the parachute risers, look at the horizon, and when my feet hit the water, release myself from the parachute so that I could get out from under it without getting trapped in deep water.

I was prepared to descend into deep water. The funny thing is, when I hit the water, I wasn't submerged—because it was only about a foot deep.

When I stood up, a young lady from Holland who lived in the subdivision came running out to the pond, asking, "Can I help you?"

I asked her to take care of my parachute because I had to go find Russ. I didn't know if he was hurt or what had happened.

I ran up the hill and, as I did, I saw Russ running down the hill to find me. We realized that nobody had died in the crash—not us, and not anybody in the residential area either.

THE FIVE C'S IN ACTION

Although I didn't know it at the time, those Five C's of Collaboration played a role in my still being alive to this day.

We were so well trained that—in an emergency situation, before ever speaking a word—we were *committed* to resolving the problem, to safely ejecting from the aircraft, since we were below the minimum ejection altitude. I was *clear* on what to do—my sole objectives were to notify Russ of the situation and to pull the ejection handle. We had *confidence* in each other, in our training, and in the ejection system. We were *cautious* enough to follow predetermined emergency procedures, and *courageous* enough to make the decision and act.

This happened during peace time, after flying combat missions with people shooting at the plane. I certainly hadn't expected to eject that day—similar to when you got into your car and drove to work today, you probably wouldn't expect to have an accident on the way home.

They talk about getting back on the horse after being thrown. In my case, it was getting back in the airplane after ejecting. Neither Russ nor I had ever ejected before. We didn't know how we would feel getting back into the airplane, but we both wanted to prove to ourselves that we could, that nothing had changed. We wanted to know and feel, "Okay, I'm still committed to this. I'm going to go fly every day, like I always did. Everything is still clear. My confidence is not shaken—in fact, in some ways, it's even better because I've been through it, and it all worked like it's supposed to. I'm not overly cautious or scared to take off."

Our collaboration was stronger than ever because it reinforced the Five C's. Sometimes, your life really does depend on how well you work together.

MAKE IT SO

Collaboration is continuous.

If you want to have the kind of effective, efficient collaboration we've been talking about, you have to realize that collaboration is a process, not a destination—and the process never stops. Your team may disband or you may change companies, but you will always be involved in different types of collaboration.

You will have to continue to commit to work together, to

gain clarity as roles, missions, and communications change. You'll need to keep training and doing simulations to build confidence and utilize caution by having checklists and plans in place. Finally, of course, you'll need the courage to keep collaborating, to continue working together, to start the next mission or the new team.

And it just keeps growing from there.

So how do you build an effective team in the first place? This could be a team at work, or a sports team, or even a family team.

You build each component of the Five C's and get buy-in from each participant.

Commitment is all or none; one is either all-in or all-out. It's easier to commit to an organization or team with already established clarity of rules and responsibilities. This builds confidence among the participants, which is what you want on your team—confident team members who are committed, trained, and clear about what they are supposed to be doing. Be careful that you don't allow courage to precede caution, except in extreme situations. Courage without caution can be a recipe for disaster.

When the Five C's are in place in a company, leadership doesn't have to spend so much time micromanaging operations, holding workers accountable, and evaluating performance. Employees know the role they play in the success of the overall mission, and the Five C's allow teams to manage themselves.

K and I knew our jobs, and we were good at what we did. We knew the targets that were assigned to us. But we had the freedom and flexibility to plan and acquire the targets as we decided, without having to call back to the squadron for advice if the weather was bad or when the enemy was shooting at us.

In the military, this is known as Commander's Intent. Let's imagine that a commander tells his troops to take a hill from the south. When they get there, the hill is heavily defended and they can't approach it from the south safely. The goal, however, is to take the hill—the direction is not the important part of the command. If the leader sees that they can take the hill from the east, that's what they should do—*not* go back to headquarters and ask *how* they should accomplish the goal.

Once a goal is clear, leaders have to be willing to delegate the authority down to let people make the decisions about how best to accomplish that goal. This allows the entire team to be more responsive and agile and, ultimately, more successful.

If you collaborate like this, you're ultimately going to make things happen—whether that's improving your reputation so you attract better employees, making your stock price go up, or increasing productivity. You're going to get better solutions to your problems, and you're going to be able to implement them faster and more efficiently.

There are some common barriers to entry into this type of collaboration—this takes time. You can't just say, "Okay, now we're going to collaborate" and start on this level tomorrow. The payoff is not immediate. If you're doing it correctly, you will have some training to do, to help people learn how to work together and understand exactly what you want them to do. These reasons are often why people don't put the effort into collaboration in the first place.

But I think you've seen how much everybody benefits and just what is possible when we learn to work together better.

Think of your collaboration like your hand. If you open your hand and spread out your fingers individually, your hand is not very strong. If you try to break a board like that, you're just going to smack it—and maybe hurt your hand. When you bring your fingers and thumb together, though, to make a fist, your collaboration becomes much more solid and you can punch right through a board.

A FINAL WORD ON GLOBAL COLLABORATION IN THE TIME OF CORONAVIRUS

Remember our model of a house as a metaphor for collaboration, from chapter 1? Well, some of our houses are on the brink of collapsing, as a result of this global pandemic. We find similar situations, whether we are looking at our global house, our national house, our state house, our city as a house, our community as a house, our business as a house, our sports teams as houses, our churches as houses—or even the actual houses we live in.

If we don't find a vaccine soon, our global house could collapse. The world economy could be in trouble and nations may be pitted against each other. The media has reported that China put out a false rumor that the coronavirus came from the United States. America holds China responsible, but it can't decide if the virus originated in a Chinese lab or in the wet market where live animals are sold. We need to put our political, economic, and cultural differences aside and work toward finding a cure and treatment that works for all nations.

In our national house of America, partisan politics may be our downfall. Both parties are committed, but not always to the same goals and roles. While we do agree on the mission, such as lowering the death rate, flattening the curve, and restarting the economy, we disagree on how to achieve our goals and the roles of the federal government, the individual states, and even the counties and cities within those states.

Our states are at odds with the federal government and cooperation is sparing, at best. They can't agree on who is responsible for what. States claim that the government should supply ventilators in a crisis, and the White House has a different viewpoint. Some states are having serious financial problems, and some politicians believe that they should be allowed to go bankrupt. Supply chains are being disrupted, food is going to waste in fields and slaughterhouses, all while food banks are running out of food and the waiting lines are often several miles long.

Cities and state officials are not always on the same page about what to do in this pandemic. There are major differences of opinions on testing, treatment, and tracing. We seem to forget that we should be the *United* States of America. Abraham Lincoln was right, "A house divided against itself, cannot stand."

Against this background, too many Black lives are being taken due to police brutality. Hundreds of thousands of people have joined protests around the globe to declare that Black Lives Matter—all while facing tear gas, rubber bullets, police in riot gear, and a deadly virus that continues to spread. Some cities and states have taken up the discussion of race relations and moved to defund or dismantle police forces, while others have dug in further and approved funding for budgets that far outpace education, outreach, social services, or other humanitarian efforts that build on the concepts of collaboration, not choke holds.

There are also problems in some of the houses where we live. Kids are getting on parents' nerves and want to go outside and play. Parents are struggling with schooling from home. Couples are having to decide on how to go back to the office, because the schools are still closed. On the other hand, they are concerned with the safety of their children when they return to school, if there is no vaccine. Spousal abuse is increasing. People in abusive situations are trapped, unable to find alternate shelter in a time when people are either suspicious of strangers or flagrantly disregard the common courtesy of wearing a mask when in public.

All of our communities and houses need help. Our businesses need to reopen, but cautiously and profitably. Stimulus monies need to get to the proper small businesses. Many Americans want their sports teams to start playing. We miss Friday night football, the PGA, the NBA, the NFL, the NHL, the MLB, March Madness, and other college competitions. Churches need to reopen. Employees who are furloughed or laid off need to get back to work. We need to restart the national economy. But none of this should be at the expense of significant increases in the loss of human lives.

This may sound bleak, but I also want to share that in recent weeks, I have seen people working together more than at any other time during my seventy-five years on earth. From families having online Zoom meetings to the worldwide effort to find a vaccine to combat the coronavirus, collaboration is on everyone's minds. Democrats and Republicans worked together to pass two multitrillion dollar bipartisan stimulus packages; over 90 percent of America has adjusted to some form of a stay-at home-order; individuals are making masks at home for others; one company is making masks from baseball uniform materials; Ford, GE Healthcare, and a British vacuum cleaner company are making ventilators; states are sending excess equipment to other states with dire needs; and other businesses and individuals are making financial contributions to the efforts of others. Bill Gates is funding research to find a vaccine in record time; the MLB gave $1 million per team for laid off workers; the New England Patriots and the Kraft family collaborated with the governor to fly over one million N95 masks from China to the States and sent 300,000 of them to NYC.

Look back at the image of our house of collaboration in chapter 1. Right now, the foundation is cracking, the walls are weak, and they can't support the roof. There is a lack of commitment, clarity, and confidence. Therefore, caution and courage can't be supported. We must fix our houses so that we can get together, work together, and be *better* together.

To find solutions to the problems generated by the pandemic, we need the following:

1. Commitment to finding proper preventive guidelines, treatment methods, and a vaccine
2. Clarity of goals and roles among countries, businesses, and organizations, with a complete and truthful sharing of all information
3. Confidence that we can depend on each other until it is agreed that the pandemic is over
4. Caution as we test and develop treatments and a vaccine
5. Courage to spend the necessary monies, provide the required resources, and move as quickly and as reasonably as is possible

Let's collaborate as if our lives depend on it—because they do.

IT STARTS NOW

As you begin any collaboration, ask these five questions:

- What commitment do we need to make?
- What do we need clarity on?
- What do we need confidence in?
- What should we show caution about?
- And what do we need courage for?

Take these principles and determine what you need to do, with the knowledge that the Five C's apply anywhere two or more people are working together.

EXERCISE

Here are some additional questions to ask yourself and your team as you work better together:

- Do you have a need in your organization for successful collaboration?
- What would an efficient and effective team look like in your organization?
- Do you value collaboration in your organization? If so, as the leader, what have you done to foster collaboration in your team or in your organization? Have you been successful? If so, how do you measure success?

- What are your internal cultural barriers to working together successfully as a team?
- What will your team look like when the Five C's are operable? How will that be different from how it currently operates?
- As a leader, to whom should the responsibility for collaboration and implementing the Five C's be given in your organization?
- What training on collaboration have you provided to your team members? Do you think training would be beneficial?
- Could you have a collaborative workshop utilizing the book to implement the Five C's?
- Ask questions like, "How can this team fail?" or, "What will make this team succeed?" Debate, switch positions, and debate again.
- Does your team operate differently when everything is going well versus when things are falling apart, livelihoods are on the line, and leadership and stakeholders are depending on the team for a solution?
- Are you willing to put the total responsibility, for whatever is on the line, in the hands of your team members or teammate(s)? Are they willing to do the same with you?
- When you look in the mirror, is the person you see an example of one who operates utilizing the Five C's?

Your chances of being successful in whatever area (or areas) you choose to collaborate in are now substantially higher. You are in a better position to accomplish your goals and go from surviving to thriving. You can have a happier marriage. Your company's bottom line can improve, or you can better your chance for promotion. Your team can win more games. And, overall, you are going to feel a lot better about what you're doing.

If you get stuck, if you need someone to help you walk through these questions, or if you need any other assistance with your collaboration, you can reach out to me. I'll let you know how we can work together to be better together.

Even though your life may not depend on collaborating, as mine did when I flew combat in Vietnam, my hope is that the implementation of the Five C's will be just as beneficial to you as they have been to me.

Again, your life may not literally depend upon working together to be better together, but living the very best life possible does.

Let's be better, together.

ABOUT THE AUTHOR

DOUG CRAWLEY serves as president and CEO of Synasha and Staffing Synergies. He is responsible for the overall planning, directing, organizing, and controlling of the company operations for both entities. He has over forty years of management and related entrepreneurial and military leadership experience. He has served as an executive for two Fortune 100 companies and has previous packaging experience as executive vice president of a multi division filling and distribution company. In addition, he has served as president of several other entrepreneurial and nonprofit entities. Doug is the founder and a volunteer of the MOST (Mentoring Our Students Together) Program, which is an after-school collaboration between his church and the local school district to provide mentoring, tutoring, and recreational activities for students in grades four through twelve.

Doug is a veteran who served as a navigator/flight instructor in the U.S. Air Force and was discharged with the rank of Captain. During his seven years of military leadership, he flew 185 combat missions during the Vietnam Conflict. Doug brings the discipline, character, and honor that earned him the Distinguished Flying Cross, the Meritorious Service Medal, the Air Force Commendation Medal, and the Air Medal.

Doug holds a Bachelor of Arts degree in Mathematics, an MBA, and a Doctor of Ministry degree.

He is a pastor, serial entrepreneur, black belt, basketball player, management consultant, real estate developer, husband, father, and grandfather.